CHAMPAGNE
& SPARKLING
WINES

Michael Edwards

Champagne & Sparkling Wine
by Michael Edwards

First published in Great Britain in 1998 by Mitchell Beazley
an imprint of Octopus Publishing Group Limited
2-4 Heron Quays, London E14 4JP

Reprinted 1999

ISBN 1 84000 077 5

A CIP catalogue record for this book is available from the British Library.

The author and publishers will be grateful for any information which will
assist them in keeping future editions up to date. Although all reasonable
care has been taken in the preparation of this book, neither the publishers
nor the author can accept responsibility for any consequences arising from
the use thereof or from the information contained therein.

Commissioning Editor: Sue Jamieson
Executive Art Editor: Fiona Knowles
Editor: Hilary Lumsden
Production: Rachel Lynch

Typeset in Veljovic

Printed and bound by Cayfosa, Spain

Acknowledgements

All credit for the sections on Germany, and on Australia and
South Africa, goes respectively to Stuart Pigott and Stuart
Walton, who wrote these pages far more convincingly than I
could ever do. I have learnt much from the writings of Burton
Anderson on Italy. My greatest debt is to my friend, Dr Teresa
Challoner, who always found time in her life as a busy
physician to read the text and save me from many infelicities.

Contents

Introduction

At the end of the 20th century, there are more good Champagnes available to the consumer than ever before. One uses the plural noun "Champagnes" deliberately here, for this is a subject of endless diversity, belying the strong brand images of around 20 *grandes marques* which dominate the wine shelves of the high street and shopping malls. It is, of course, quite natural that busy consumers should remain brand loyal to the style of a great Champagne house they particularly like. So, a good part of the Directory of producers' Champagne section of this book seeks to distinguish the differing styles of the *grandes marques*, sorting the true "greats" from the merely good.

Yet, beyond the magic circle of the big names, there is a huge number of Champagnes made by large cooperatives and small growers in every conceivable style, to suit all tastes and budgets. A Champagne can be a Blanc de Blancs, made only from Chardonnay; a Blanc de Noirs, produced from either of the two Pinots or both; a blend of white and black grapes in any proportion; from a single *cru* or from 200; non vintage or vintage; aged on lees for a few months or for many years; barely dosed or strongly sugared; disgorged early or late. Nearly all these elements can be subtly changed and varied, and the main purpose of this guide is to point you to the producers, famous or lesser known, who play to the peak of Champagne's aptitude to be the most complex and long-lived sparkling wine in the world.

Unusually, over 170 small *récoltants-manipulants* (grower-Champagne-makers) are profiled – the best of them are the true guardians of quality today and produce remarkably individual wines that deserve wider recognition.

The Champagne producers do not have a monopoly of excellence in this field. One great satisfaction of working on this project has been to discover sparkling-winemakers around the world who are as much driven perfectionists as the most meticulous *chef de caves* in Reims or Epernay.

The *crémant* producers of Alsace in particular have made great strides in recent years, creating bottle-fermented sparklers that extend the taste spectrum of the *genre* by the use of their own noble grape varieties such as Pinot Gris and Riesling alongside Pinot Noir, and maybe even a little Chardonnay. Across the Alps in Italy's Lombardy region, the wealthy estate owners of Franciacorta have created, in Burton Anderson's words, "a miniature Champagne on the shores of Lake Isea". It is interesting to note that the DOCG laws governing the making of Franciacorta are the toughest for any sparkling wine in the world – the youngest wine in the *cuvée*, for example, must be aged on lees for a minimum of 25 months.

Down under in Australia – improved technology, carefully chosen vineyard sites and imported expertise from, for example, Moët & Chandon, have all helped transform their sparkling wines. With rare exceptions, they may not taste much like the real thing, but they have an easy fruit-laden character that will win many friends.

South Africa has made extraordinary progress in less than ten years – their best Méthode-Cap-Classique sparklers show a rich, creamy complexity that is easy to confuse with a well-aged vintage Champagne.

The cool Marlborough district, in the South Island of New Zealand, is a natural environment in which to grow Pinot Noir and Chardonnay grapes with that verve and "tension" essential to high-class sparkling winemaking. Results are already impressive, and quite conceivably Marlborough could become the capital of fizz in the southern hemisphere by the early years of the next century, eclipsing its newly won international reputation for still Sauvignon Blanc.

West, to the North American continent, in the coolest parts of California's Mendocino County; Oregon; and the Hudson Valley in New York State, are climates and latitudes similar to that of Champagne, and sparkling wines are produced that would not be shamed in any company.

Happy hunting – keep an open mind, and you will be in for some pleasant surprises in all categories, and for all occasions!

How to use this book

The first and major part of this book is a study of Champagne in all its aspects. An introductory history of the wine, the land and the people concludes with an overview of the industry today. The million dollar question, "What makes a great Champagne?", is answered by a close look at the special character of the place – grapes, climate, rocks and soils.

A detailed account of the Champagne-making process is followed by an analysis of the structure of the Champagne trade. There are practical tips on understanding the label on a bottle of Champagne; storing, opening and serving the wine; plus how to keep an unfinished bottle in good condition. This leads on to special features on matching the wine with food, and what to buy for the millennium.

The second part of this book is a region-by-region gazetteer directory of 500 major sparkling-wine producers around the world. Each region has an introduction describing the wines and, where appropriate, aspects of their history and production to help the reader know what style of sparkler to expect. Each entry has a bold-typed heading with the name of the producer, his address and an overall quality "star-rating" system (*see* below). The text profiles producers, highlighting their winemaking philosophy, and particular wines (*cuvées*) worth seeking out. The entries and emphases are largely based on my own experiences and preferences (entirely so in the case of Champagne), but I have tried to weigh my judgements against those of other tasters and critics I respect.

A helpful glossary of technical terms; a Champagne vintage guide from 1997 back to 1900; and information about Champagne's gastronomy are found at the end of the book.

The quality rating of each entry is denoted by stars as follows:
☆ decent
☆☆ good to very good
☆☆☆ excellent, much admired
☆☆☆☆ outstanding

A number of abbreviations have been used throughout this book. Vineyard areas, in Europe especially, are expressed in hectares (shortened to ha) and grape yields in hectolitres (hl) or hectolitres per hectare (hl/ha).
AOC Appellation d'Origine Contrôlée (France)
DO Denominación de Origen (Spain)
DOC Denominazione di Origine (Italy)
DOCG Demoninazio di Origine e Garantita (Italy)
1 hectare (ha) = 2.47 acres
1 hectolitre (hl) = 100 litres, or 21.997 imperial gallons, or 26.45 US gallons

A history of Champagne

Historians tend to date the beginning of the Champagne wine story from the rise of the Frankish kings in the 5th-century AD. We know that Saint Rémi, Bishop of Reims baptised King Clovis on Christmas Day 496. Legend has it that Rémi gave Clovis a barrel of blessed wine, and recommended that as long as he drank his daily ration from the sanctified cask he would vanquish his enemies. Champagne's royal associations were greatly strengthened in 987, when Hugh Capet was crowned French King in the cathedral at Reims. This established that city, rather than Paris, as the spiritual capital of medieval France. Subsequently, 37 of Capet's successors came to Reims for their coronations, the last being Charles X in 1825.

The special relationship that Reims had with the monarchy was the impetus for an expansion of the vineyards. Successive kings made generous gifts of land to the numerous abbeys around Reims and in the Marne Valley. These quickly became excellent winemaking institutions. The position of the Champagne wine region at the crossroads of two major trade routes of northern Europe brought it prosperity, but also made it vulnerable to attack by invaders, mainly from the east. The wine town of Epernay, for example, was sacked 25 times between the seventh and sixteenth centuries and was devastated again during the Fronde, the dreadful French civil war of the 1640s and 1650s. But on Louis XIV's accession to the throne at the age of 16 in 1654, the canny Champenois made a present of their wines to the young king. He liked them so much that they became his preferred drink.

Until the mid-17th-century, the notion of a generic *vin de Champagne* did not exist. As early as the ninth century, drinkers had made a distinction between the wines from vineyards bordering the Marne Valley and those from the slopes of the Montagne de Reims. The latter, more pink than white, and made entirely from black grapes, but both were regarded as "still" wines. Yet by the early 1600s the more observant monks noted that the wines of Champagne had a natural tendency to sparkle. The bitter northern climate – the autumns and winters in Champagne were much colder then than they are now – meant that the grapes were usually picked before they were fully ripe, so the wines tended to be high in acid and low in alcohol – properties that caused them to fizz. Moreover, wines that started their fermentation in cask and finished it in a sealed, albeit fragile, glass bottle (first made around 1630) released carbonic gas which had no means of escape; hence the bubbles.

Paradoxically, a sparkling Champagne of sorts was probably first drunk in England to celebrate the ending of the hated Commonwealth rule of Oliver Cromwell and the restoration of the Stuart kings (1660). English merchants from this time used to import the wines of Champagne in cask after the harvest and bottle them themselves the following spring. With the creation of the sturdy, thick-bodied bottle by the London glaziers Holden and Colenet in 1662, John Bull had a head start over Marianne in the cork popping business. The Restoration playwright Sir George Etheredge in *The Man of Fashion* (1672) has his comic character Flopping voice a celebration of "effervescent Champagne which quickly revives the poor languishing lovers, makes them happy and gay, and chases away their woes".

Meanwhile, winemaking was greatly improving in the Marne Valley area of Champagne, especially at the Abbey of Hautvillers under the aegis of Dom Pérignon, head cellarer there from 1668 to 1715. Dom Pérignon has been called the inventor of sparkling Champagne. That a teetotal monk could have created the world's most sybaritic wine, associated with seduction and dissipation, makes a fine story, but it is a myth. In the words of Nicholas Faith, Dom Pérignon was "simply one of the most distinguished evolutionaries in developing the wines of Champagne". His great achievement was to make a clear still white wine from black grapes, and he was almost certainly the first to grasp that, in the bleak conditions of the Champagne country, there was a much better chance of making a palatable, balanced drink by blending wines from different vineyards. The fact that the wines sparkled was probably a nuisance, which Dom Pérignon tried to control rather than encourage. Throughout the 18th century, serious connoisseurs preferred their Champagne still; it was the fops and ladies of the Regency court at Versailles who liked to lubricate their *louche* supper parties with *vin mousseux*.

The first half of the 19th century saw the foundation of the sparkling-Champagne trade as we know it today. In the early 1800s, the Champagne makers profited from Napoleon's military success in Austria, Prussia and Poland. Wherever the Emperor was victorious, a Champagne salesman appeared to offer the locals his wine and set up a network of contacts for future business. Jean-Rémy Moët, the greatest merchant of his day, expanded his Champagne firm (founded in 1743) through his friendship with Napoleon. Today, opposite Moët's offices on Epernay's Avenue de Champagne stands the Trianon, twin white pavilions with a formal sunken garden and orangery, which Jean-Rémy built to lodge Napoleon's court on its marches to and from the battlefields of eastern Europe. And yet, even by the time of Waterloo, making sparkling Champagne was still a crude and chancy business.

The deposit formed inside the bottle (the by-product of the secondary fermentation) could be removed only by decanting the contents into a new bottle – a messy and prohibitively expensive operation for a sparkling wine. Plus, the adding of sugar to induce the wine to sparkle vigorously frequently resulted in too much pressure inside the bottle, causing it to explode.

There were two inventions in the 19th century that solved these problems. In 1818 Antoine Muller, cellar-master at Veuve Clicquot, developed the system of *pupitres* to facilitate the process of *remuage* – shifting the angle of the bottle in order to make the deposit gravitate towards the cork (*see* page 16). The *pupitres* were inverted-V-shaped desks with holes in them. The bottles were placed neck-down in the holes so that they could be turned and tilted every day until the deposit settled on the cork. The second great invention was a tool called the *sucréoenometre* (a wine-sugar measure) created in 1836 by André François, a young pharmacist from Châlons-sur-Marne. This accurately measured the residual sugar in the still wine prior to its second fermentation. With this crucial piece of apparatus the Champagne maker could add just the right amount of extra sugar to the wine to make it sparkle without generating too much pressure inside the bottle. From this date sparkling Champagne, reliably produced in commercial quantities, came of age. Within a generation of François' premature death in 1838, Champagne had become an international business on an industrial scale. With the plethora of cut-price Champagnes of poor quality and questionable origin that inevitably attended this boom in sales, a positive result was the emergence of famous Champagne "brands" on which the drinker could rely.

Several of the best brand names were established by immigrants from the German Rhineland who, between 1827 and 1843, founded firms such as Bollinger, Mumm, Krug and Deutz & Geldermann. Adept at speaking foreign languages, these newcomers were better able to penetrate world markets than the older local houses, many of which had disappeared by 1850.

Until the middle of the 19th century, all Champagne was given a hefty dose of sugared *liqueur* in order to make the essentially acid-wine drinkable within a year or two of the vintage. But following the lead of Perrier-Jouët in 1848, a few firms by the 1860s were reducing the dose of *liqueur* in their wines in response to a new trend, fostered by the British, towards a drier and more mature type of Champagne. Ayala and Bollinger both shipped their "very dry" 1865 vintage to England; both wines were said to have converted the Prince of Wales, the future Edward VII, to the pleasures of Champagne, though neither was naturally brut (bone-dry) by modern standards.

The first truly dry Champagne was the 1874 of Pommery & Greno, which took Victorian London by storm in 1878. Within a few years, the house of Mumm was selling 900,000 bottles of bubbly a year in the USA – its best outlets were the luxurious brothels of New Orleans, where wine literally meant Champagne. Between 1850 and 1900 total exports of Champagne quadrupled from five to twenty million bottles.

For well over 50 years into the 20th century the region of Champagne was blighted by a series of crises that unfortunately cast a dark shadow over its earlier achievements. By 1905 the feared *phylloxera* aphid had devastated the vineyards of the Marne Valley, causing a drastic loss of income for the Champenois growers. Further still, these growers resented the unprincipled merchants who were fraudulently buying grapes for their *cuvées* from well outside the classic wine districts of Champagne. When the French government included the Aube, a separate region 160 kilometres south of Reims, within the Champagne grape-growing zone in 1911, the Marnois producers rioted and civil war was only narrowly avoided.

During the First World War, the Reims area was nearly destroyed by German artillery and the city had to be completely rebuilt after 1918. Subsequently, the bleak puritanical mood that followed the Armistice was a sinister portent. The important Russian market had already disappeared in the Bolshevik revolution of 1917, and the USA went dry with the advent of Prohibition in 1920. Then came the Wall Street Crash of 1929 and the resulting great depression of the early 1930s.

With the ending of Prohibition in 1933, the Champagne industry started to recover, thanks largely to the vision of Robert-Jean de Vogüé, the head of Moët & Chandon, who proposed that the price of Champagne grapes be increased sixfold to ensure a decent living for the growers. And during the Second World War, again on de Vogüé's initiative, the German occupying powers were persuaded to establish the Comité Interprofessionnel du Vin de Champagne (CIVC) as the governing body of the industry – both as referee and player – arbitrating between the competing claims of growers and merchants, and also acting as a skilled publicity machine for the Champagne trade.

The CIVC has since become one of the most effective official wine organisations in France.

A REFORMED INDUSTRY

In the 40 years after 1950, the region enjoyed great prosperity with sales quadrupling to 200 million bottles a year. But in a twist of fortune that is so regular a feature of this story, the early 1990s was a time of trauma in Champagne.

After a long bullish trading period, until 1989, during which prices soared way above the real demands of the market, the industry was stricken by the worst economic crisis since the 1930s. The sharp fall in sales lead to a collapse in prices and a swelling of stocks, compounded by seven bumper crops between 1989 and 1996. Every type of Champagne producer – house, cooperative, grower – was hit hard and huge losses were incurred.

When viewed from the late 1990s, the worst is over. The Champagne economy is out of danger but it will need a period of convalescence to restore it to good health. Catastrophe has been avoided by draconian measures, initiated by the Champagne authorities in 1992, to reduce yields in the vineyard and improve procedures for the pressing of the harvest – a critical stage in Champagne making.

The wines are now generally aged for longer on lees – three to four years for a non-vintage and five to six for a vintage from a good house. Happily the result is a leap in quality in the finished wines.

What makes a great Champagne

Several of the world's finest fruits are grown in cold climates where the plants have to struggle to survive. Witness English apples and Scottish raspberries. It also seems that, at the extreme limit of its culture, the vine yields grapes that are particularly delicate and pure in flavour – the perfect raw material for making exquisitely refined yet fruity white wines such as Chablis, Moselle and, of course, Champagne. It is this restrained exuberance of flavour that sets Champagne apart from lesser sparkling wines – its distinction shaped by its total natural environment.

THE PLACE

Centred on the cathedral city of Reims and the wine town of Epernay, the classic heartland of Champagne Viticole lies about 90 miles northeast of Paris on the road to the Belgian border. The three principal wine-growing districts are the Montagne de Reims, the Vallée de la Marne and the Côte des Blancs. About 100-miles south of Reims, the Aube is also part of Champagne, even if the terrain more resembles Burgundy (Chablis is just a 40-minute drive from Bar-sur-Seine, a central Aubois wine commune). Champagne grapes are also grown across the Aisne towards Paris, and in isolated pockets within Seine-et-Marne and Haute-Marne.

The winefield covers 34,000 hectares, of which 31,000 are currently planted. It is situated on the 49th parallel (latitude), and these are the most northerly fine wine vineyards in France. So, frosty springs, variable summers and treacherous autumns pose potential problems to the quality and quantity of the grapes produced. Quite astonishingly, the well-drained chalky subsoils of the Champagne heartland provide enough protection from the elements for the classic grape varieties to produce juice which is rich in acids and sugar – the defining characteristic of a great sparkling wine.

THE GRAPES

Three grapes dominate the vineyards of Champagne. Pinot Noir, representing 37·5 per cent of total production, is planted mainly on the chalky, sandy hillsides of the Montagne de Reims, giving wines of richness and finesse. It is also the most important grape of the Aube, where it covers four-fifths of its vineyard area.

The hardy Pinot Meunier is more suited to the colder, frost-prone soils of the Vallée de la Marne, where it dependably produces regular crops of early maturing, fruity wine with a hint of spice – an essential and attractive component in a well-balanced non-vintage Champagne. It is an important part of the Champagne culture, accounting for 35 per cent of the winefield area. The Chardonnay grape flourishes in the deep Belimnite chalk of the Côte des Blancs.

Fortunately, less prone to frost damage than the Pinot Noir, Chardonnay also ripens earlier and has a higher yield. It is delicate and fresh, with great aromatic potential, and is a vital component in the finer Champagne blends providing verve to balance the richness of Pinot Noir. A Blanc de Blancs Champagne is one made from pure Chardonnay. Briskly refreshing and incisive, it makes a perfect *apéritif*, but when sourced from the greatest Chardonnay vineyards and allowed to age for ten years it develops opulent flavours of butter, hazelnuts and cream, more akin to a fine still white burgundy than to a conventional sparkling wine.

THE ASPECT, ROCKS AND SOILS

The classic wine-growing districts are located in that part known as the *falaises* or chalky cliffs of Champagne. Chalk is something of a religion for Champagne growers, especially those who own parcels in the most highly rated vineyards. However, chalk can be exaggerated as the only element that matters is the structure of the soil.

In my opinion, the great Champagne writer Patrick Forbes was certainly overstating the case when he wrote, "only when there are seams of Belimnite chalk will the vines produce radiant crops on the *falaises*, and grapes that can be turned into Champagne, which has Champagne's unique, inimitable flavour". Such a claim can be made for the finest sites of the Côte des Blancs, especially those in Le Mesnil, but it is far too sweeping a generalisation to apply to the totality of the Champagne winefield, whose geology is much more complicated and varied than that implies.

The great Pinot Noir vineyards of the Montagne de Reims are a case in point. These sites have varying amounts of sand, marl and lignite clay as well as two types of chalk in their soil structure. It is the interplay of all these elements that makes the wines special. In an area covering 7,000 hectares of vines, the wine villages of the Montagne de Reims are a heterogeneous mix and offer a wide palate of flavours. The superb north-facing vineyards of Verzenay, for example, reputedly produce the blackest grapes and the strongest wines, while Trépail at the extreme southeast tip of the Montagne de Reims is known for fruity, early maturing Chardonnay and Pinot Noir. On the south side, the great sites of Ambonnay, Bouzy and Aÿ produce richly textured Pinots of superb harmony of flavour.

Into the Vallée de la Marne, the further west you go, the heavier and less chalky the soil becomes. This is Pinot Meunier country where, contrary to what you might expect, the quality of the grapes scarcely varies whether the vineyards face north or south – an instance where a hardier workhorse variety like Pinot Meunier works better in the clay soils than Pinot Noir would.

The Côte des Blancs, beginning just east of Epernay in the Grands Crus of Chouilly and Oiry, is a barrier of east-facing hills which extends south for 11 miles to the Mont Aimé. The vineyards, on a deep stratum of Belimnite and Micraster chalk, are more homogeneous than those of the Montagne de Reims and produce Chardonnays of the highest class. The different flavours of each wine village are subtle: Cramant is very aromatic; Avize pure; Oger all delicacy; Le Mesnil powerful and long lived.

The Côte de Sézanne is an extension of the Côte des Blancs, but is separated from the latter by the marshes of St-Gond. The chalky soils and the favourable southeast aspect of the Sézannais make it ideal for the production of good Chardonnay grapes, which display rounded, forward, slightly rustic flavours.

The Aube is different again. Here the soil is composed largely of Kimmeridgian and Portlandian limestone, also found in northern Burgundy and Sancerre, so Pinot Noir is the ideal grape to produce splendid *rosé* wines, both still and sparkling, that are the glories of the district. Chalk (of yet another type called Tironian) resurfaces on the great south-facing hill of Montgueux, found just west of Troyes. This is the capital of the Aube; and the soft, golden and fruity, Montgueux Chardonnay can be a sumptuous component in a Champagne blend.

As the *chef de caves* at Veuve Clicquot will tell you, great Champagne is an intricate tapestry of many threads.

Classification of vineyards and grape prices

As the sales of Champagne grew in the golden age of expansion between 1850 and the first years of the 20th century, so it became necessary to create a hierarchy of places where Champagne grapes could be grown. In 1919, all the wine-growing villages of Champagne's Marne Valley heartland were classified on a percentage scale known as *l'échelle des crus* (the "ladder" of growths).

In 1927 the vineyards of the Aube region, as part of an enlarged Champagne winefield, were also classified. Although geographically based, the *échelle* is essentially an index of price, graded on the reputed quality of grapes from particular communes. The Grands Crus rate 100 per cent; the Premiers Crus rate 90–99 per cent; and the Deuxièmes Crus rate 80–89 per cent (*see* page 14 for individual village ratings). For 30 years, starting in 1959, the CIVC announced the annual fixed price per kilo of grapes destined to become Champagne.

VINEYARD RATING (%)

Montagne de Reims

Ambonnay	100
Beaumont-sur-Vesle	100
Bouzy	100
Chigny-les-Roses	94
Louvois	100
Ludes	94
Mailly	100
Puisieulx	100
Rilly-La-Montagne	94
Sillery	100
Tauxières	99
Trépail	95
Verzenay	100
Verzy	100
Villers-Marmery	95

Vallée de la Marne

Avenay	93
Aÿ	100
Bisseuil	95
Champillon	93
Cumières	93
Dizy	95
Hautvillers	93
Mareuil-sur-Aÿ	99
Mutigny	93
Tours-sur-Marne	100

Vallée du Cubry (Marne Valley Tributary)

Cuis	95
Grauves	95
Pierry	90

Côte des Blancs

Avize	100
Bergères-les-Vertus	95
Chouilly	100
Cramant	100
Le Mesnil-sur-Oger	100
Oger	100
Oiry	100
Vertus	95

This indicated the price of grapes from 100-per-cent-rated vineyards, while the grapes from lesser-rated vineyards commanded lower prices in line with their exact rating on the index. Thus, if the announced fixed price for the 100-per-cent-rated Grand Cru of Aÿ was ten *francs*, then that for the 94-per-cent-rated Premier Cru of Ludes would be 9.4 *francs*.

In April 1990, after months of negotiation, the Champagne growers and merchants failed to renew their contract with the CIVC. The result was that, in principle at least, the Champagne houses were free to negotiate the price of grapes directly with the growers. The reality of grape price negotiations in the 1990s has been a compromise between the old, annual, fixed-price system and a market free-for-all. Regulation of the grape market now progressively rests on a three- to four-year contract system between seller and buyer.

A new accord was reached in the spring of 1996 concerning the price of grapes for the vintages '96, '97, '98 and '99, allowing a maximum annual rise of only one *franc* per kilo. However, the *échelle* system remains intact as the chief yardstick for determining the differential of grape prices in Champagne. Like all vineyard classifications, the *échelle* is not perfect. Its main weakness is that it makes no qualitative distinction between individual vineyard sites within the same *cru* category. Furthermore, it obviously cannot take account of the all-important human factor. Clearly, a talented grower producing ripe 80-per-cent-rated Chardonnay grapes in Montgueux is a surer source of supply than an incompetent grower producing sour 100-per-cent-rated fruit in Le Mesnil. Champagne may be a blend, but it is only as good as the grapes from which it is made – just like any truly fine wine.

The leading vineyards of the classic Champagne Viticole heartland with their percentage ratings are listed on page 14.

The Champagne process

At every stage of the Champagne-making process, from grape to glass, the primary aim is to protect the wine's freshness, cleanness and purity of flavour. At harvest time grape-picking machines are prohibited; all harvesting must be done by hand. This is because Champagne is the product of white wine made mainly from black grapes – the two Pinots – and it is imperative that the neutral-coloured juice should not be put in contact with the outer surface of the black skins, which would tint it. After picking, the pressing must be put into effect quickly – by the '96 vintage, more than 2,000 pressing centres had been registered across the area, minimising the distances involved in transporting the grapes.

The grapes are pressed gently either in the traditional vertical wooden *coquard* presses or in pneumatic ones, which hold 4,000 kilos at a time. This gives 2,500 litres of juice, obtained by two pressings. The first, the *cuvée*, produces 2,050 litres; the second, the *taille*, 450 litres. There used to be a third pressing but this was officially abolished in 1992, and a good thing too, for with each successive pressing the "must" (pressed juice and grape matter) becomes successively darker and more tannic, and so less desirable. In practice, the best firms tend to use only the *cuvée*, plus the best part of the *taille* from Chardonnay grapes for extra body and fruitiness. The rest of the *taille* is usually sold off to firms who produce cheap Champagne and whose requirements are less exacting.

After the pressing, impurities in the must are eliminated by *débourbage*, a cleansing process which allows solid matter to fall to the bottom of the vat over 12 to 24 hours. James Coffinet, the distinguished *chef de caves* formerly at Billecart-Salmon, now at Pol Roger, has perfected a system involving a "cold settling" of the must at very low temperatures. This greatly enhances the purity of flavour in the finished Champagne. The clear juice then goes through its first fermentation, which usually takes place in stainless steel tanks. A few great houses such as Krug, Jacquesson and Bollinger (vintage wines) still ferment in wood, as do perfectionist growers such as René Geoffroy, Anselme Selosse and Jean-Mary Tarlant.

THE CHAMPAGNE METHOD

Méthode Champenoise, or *méthode traditionelle* as Brussels insists it is now called, is the name for the process of making a still wine sparkle by allowing it to ferment for a second time in the bottle. It is now used to make good sparkling wine around the world.

Outside Champagne, other producers of sparkling wine would have us believe that it is only the method that matters, but what really matters is the wine and, as we have seen, Champagne is unique. The skill of the blender puts it into a separate class. Blending requires taste, experience and, above all, memory. Each January, the *chef de caves* starts to compose his non-vintage *cuvée*. He and his team will taste hundreds of still wines, eventually arriving at a selection of those that marry well, consistent with the established style of the house. The *chef de caves* will also call on reserve wines from older vintages to make up for any deficiencies in the present one. Thus, in the best hands, a technical function is elevated into an art form.

Once the blend is assembled, the *liqueur de tirage* (yeasts, old wine and sugar) is added and the wine bottled. The slow process known as the *prise de mousse* will produce a persistent stream of tiny bubbles. The second fermentation takes place in the deepest and coolest part of the cellar at a constant temperature of 10–12°C (50–54°F), with the bottles binned *sur lattes* (on their sides). Deposits are formed, mostly of dead yeasts (lees), which add complexity to the wine's flavour. Much of the process – the creation of lively bubbles in the wine – appears to be over within two to three weeks. But the final stages, retarded by the pressure of the fizz, can last as long as three months, especially for the finer *cuvées*.

The top traditionalist house of Ruinart, for example, prefers the wine to have extended contact with the deposit *sur lattes*, because when the bottle is in this horizontal position, a greater surface area of the wine is touched by the yeasts and more vinous flavours are developed.

REMOVING THE DEPOSIT

Remuage is a process used to remove the yeast deposits. The equivalent term in English is "riddling". Traditionally, the bottles are placed in holed racks called *pupitres* and are turned and tilted every day, eventually arriving at an almost vertical position, neck downward. This induces the deposit to settle on the cap or cork.

Much of this labour-intensive work is now carried out by computer-controlled machines called *gyropalettes*, which complete the job far more quickly than the skilled *remueurs* who perform the task by hand over several months. Sometimes the technology fails in the case of a particularly sticky deposit, and the *remueur* comes to the rescue. Nearly all prestige *cuvées* continue to be riddled by hand. At the next stage, the bottles are taken from the *pupitres* or *gyropalette* and stacked vertically, *sur pointes* (upside down) to mature gently for a period which can vary from a mere 60 days to many years, depending on the quality and ageing potential of the Champagne.

In any event, thus stored, they are ready for the process known as *dégorgement*. This simply means disgorging, or expelling, the sediment from the neck of the bottle. The bottles which are in an inverted vertical position, are passed along a conveyor that freezes the liquid in the neck of the bottle, trapping the sediment in a tiny "sorbet" of near-frozen wine. The bottle is then upended by the *dégorgeur*, who removes the cork, allowing the pressure of the gas to propel the slush of ice from the wine, leaving the remainder clear and bright.

This technique, invented in the Henri Abelé cellars in 1884, is known as *dégorgement à la glace*, and is now almost universally practised in the industry. The other, and older method of disgorging, *dégorgement à la volée*, involves expelling the sediment without freezing it – this is seldom used nowadays except for old Champagnes that require gentle treatment to preserve their aromas. Unavoidably, a little wine is lost during the disgorging process, and to compensate for this, an equal amount of *dosage de l'expédition* (a solution of cane sugar and still Champagne) is added to the bottle: the sugar content of this *liqueur* will affect the style of the wine and its relative sweetness.

DOSAGE: SWEETNESS AND DRYNESS

The addition of varying amounts of *liqueur*, expressed in grams of sugar per litre of wine (g/l), broadly results in the following categories of Champagne described below (from bone dry to very sweet).

Extra Brut/Ultra Brut/Brut Integral/Brut Zéro

Bone-dry Champagne to which, in principle at least, no *liqueur* is added. Instead the topping-up is done with the equivalent amount of the same wine. There is a small *niche* market for such unsweetened Champagne, which can be wonderfully refreshing on a hot summer's night. The best exponents are Laurent-Perrier, Pierre Gimmonet, Jacques Selosse and Jean-Mary Tarlant.

Brut: 1–15g/l

This offers quite a broad span, ranging from very dry to dry Champagne, depending on the style of the house (for example, Bollinger Special Cuvée is very dry, Mumm Cordon Rouge markedly less so). The best non-vintage *cuvées* are always reserved for the Brut.

Extra dry: 12–20g/l
Dry to medium-dry Champagne.

Sec: 17–35g/l
Confusingly, since Sec literally means dry, this is actually slightly sweet Champagne.

Demi-Sec: 33–50g/l
Further potential confusion here since Demi-Sec suggests half-dry, but in fact describes a medium-sweet to sweet Champagne. It can be delicious (especially Pol Roger, Lanson and Mercier) if it is not too cloying.

Doux: over 50g/l
A very sweet, dessert-style Champagne. Loved by the Russians before the 1917 revolution and, again, post 1989.

Champagne styles

The range of wines of a particular house is a good indication of the Champagne styles it offers. But, where the grapes come from and the size and age of its stocks are more precise points you should consider when deciding whether a firm can provide a Champagne style to your taste.

Such details can be checked in the firm's entry in the Directory of producers section (*see* pages 29–70). Most houses offer wines in the following styles:

Non vintage (NV)
A blend that aims to maintain the same standard, year after year. Good houses and growers offer their non-vintage *cuvée* with an age of about three years on lees. To keep your wine merchant on his toes, ask the age of the base wine (the youngest) in the blend.

Beware of cheap NV Champagne which may have only 16 months of bottle age; it will probably taste very acidic.

Vintage
The top wine of a vintage whose exceptional quality and character are considered to be too good to be lost in the non-vintage blending tanks. Good vintage Champagnes from the best houses are usually aged for seven years before release.

The truly great vintages (such as '64 and '85) do not reach their apogee until they are 15, 20, or sometimes even 25 years old.

Rosé
Pink Champagne is usually made by blending a small quantity of still red wine from one of the best Pinot Noir villages (often Aÿ or Cumières) with a larger proportion of

still white Chardonnay wine. This blend undergoes a second fermentation, which creates the bubbles. Generally this interventionist method produces fruity yet fine-drawn wine that has Champagne's essential elegance.

The other way of making pink Champagne is much more difficult – the pressed juice is put in contact with Pinot Noir grapes, the desired rose or pink hue is achieved by the colour pigments of the grape skins seeping into the wine. This sort of *rosé* Champagne tends to be much more full bodied than that made by the blending method described above, but it can be quite coarse. It is also difficult to obtain a uniform colour year after year.

Blanc de Blancs

A Champagne which is made purely from white Chardonnay grapes. It is generally brisker and more finely drawn than a classic Champagne.

Blanc de Noirs

A Champagne made from black grapes only; sometimes with a faintly pinkish tinge, always full bodied and rich.

Cuvée de Prestige

This luxury Champagne, which appears under many brand names, is made on the no-expense-spared principle. Moët & Chandon's Dom Pérignon (1935) was the first to be produced, and now most houses have one.

Though the best *cuvées de prestige* are magnificent Champagnes (especially Roederer's Cristal and Deutz's Cuvée William Deutz), many connoisseurs will argue that money is better spent buying two bottles of vintage Champagne from a good smaller firm, for the price of one *cuvée de prestige* from a large house, whose promotional budget is also built into the price of the wine.

Crémant

This is the old name for a Champagne that foams gently rather than bubbles vigorously; technically, a *crémant*-style wine has three-and-a-half atmospheres of pressure as opposed to five for a standard Champagne. These wines are excellent with subtly flavoured fish dishes.

Since 1994, the Champagne houses have been forbidden to use the word *crémant* on the front label.

Coteaux Champenois

This is the appellation for still white, *rosé* and red wines produced in Champagne Viticole; known as *vin nature de Champagne* before 1973. The white in particular has high acidity but can be exquisitely fine (especially Moët's Château de Saran).

Rosé des Riceys

A separate appellation for the rare, still *rosé* wine produced from 100-per-cent Pinot Noir grapes grown in the communes of Les Riceys in the southern Aube. It is made in tiny quantities, on average one year in three.

The seeping Pinot Noir juice macerates on essentially uncrushed grapes for three to six days until just the right light-ruby tint and characteristic *goût des Riceys* are achieved. The taste and structure of the wine – delicate yet strongly constituted – can be fascinating, and in great years such as 1990 this remarkable *rosé* can live for 30 years. The best producers are Alexandre Bonnet and Jacques Defrance.

WHO MAKES CHAMPAGNE?

Outside France, the Champagne market is dominated by the big houses. Traditionally the *élite* of these, some 23 firms, are called the *grandes marques*. However, this club of the great and the good may well disband in the late 1990s. This is the result of a disagreement among members about implementing much-needed changes in quality and stock control and the marketing of their brands, as recommended by the reforming president of the *grandes marques*, Jean-Claude Rouzaud of Louis Roederer.

The big houses own only about 13 per cent of the vineyards and rely on more than 15,000 growers to provide them with grapes. During the last 25 years, there has been a significant increase in the number of Champagnes made by the smaller *récoltants-manipulants* (grower-producers).

In 1970 there were 2,900 growers making their own Champagne; by 1997 that figure had risen to 4,100. The proportion of sales represented by the grower-producers and cooperatives had risen from 25 per cent in 1970 to 42 per cent in 1997. Most of this growth was within France, at first by direct sales and mail order to private customers, more recently by selling to high-quality fashionable restaurants. Further still, the big houses' share of the market is being increasingly challenged by cooperatives and (to a lesser extent) grower-producers, whose Champagnes, when carefully selected, can offer excellent quality at the right price.

Understanding the label

French Champagne is easy to distinguish from other sparkling wines on a shop shelf, as the real thing will simply have the name "Champagne" printed in large letters on the upper half of the label. Words such as *appellation contrôlée*, *méthode Champenoise* or *méthode traditionelle* are not mentioned, as Champagne is the only quality French wine that is not obliged to show its AOC status on the label. It is also only one of two sparkling wines in the world (the other is Franciacorta) that does not advertise its method of production, "take that as read," say the Champenois haughtily. However, a Champagne label displays a lot of information that is useful in deciding which wine to buy.

A Champagne label will always declare the wine's relative dryness or sweetness: from bone-dry Brut Zéro to unctuously sweet Doux and, where applicable a specific style such as Blanc de Noirs, Blanc de Blancs and so on. Vintage Champagnes display the vintage year of the wine (that is the year the grapes were harvested), and sometimes the date of the disgorging process (*dégorgement*). This is an increasing trend among top houses for their vintage wines. Since 1997 Charles Heidsieck has offered a range of three non-vintage *cuvées* of different ages, indicating the respective bottling dates for each *cuvée*. The quantity of wine in the bottle is declared (*see* "Champagne bottle sizes" and their equivalent liquid volumes on page 22). The alcoholic content is also declared as a percentage of liquid volume, and is normally about 12 per cent.

The producer's town or village and the word "France" (as the country of origin) are displayed on the lower half of the label. But the most intriguing item appears in tiny letters at the bottom. This is the professional registration code devised in 1990 by the CIVC. The first two letters denote the type of Champagne producer, as follows:

NM (Négociant-Manipulant)
A merchant or shipper who is allowed to buy Champagne grapes for blends from other sources. Some or all of the wines in a blend may come from the *négociant-manipulant's* own vineyards. All the *grandes marques* are NMs.

RM (Récoltant-Manipulant)
A grower making Champagne from his or her own grapes, but who is allowed to buy in five per cent from other sources.

CM (Coopérative-Manipulante)
A cooperative making and selling its own Champagne sourced from the grapes of its member growers.

SR (Société de Récoltant)
A registered enterprise which is established by Champagne growers belonging to the same family who wish to pool their production resources.

RC (Récoltant-Coopérateur)
Almost invariably a small grower who, for lack of equipment to make Champagne himself, dispatches his grapes to one or several cooperatives for "Champagnisation". The finished Champagne is then returned to him to sell. Strictly speaking,

this is not a true grower's Champagne, as his grapes will probably have been blended with others' during production.

MA (Marque d'Acheteur)

Translates as "Buyer's Own Brand" (BOB). Wines by such producers are widely used by British wine merchants, retail chains and supermarkets that require their own label, rather than that of the producer who made the Champagne for them. The quality of such wines varies widely, though the best (especially Waitrose's Blanc de Noirs) are great buys.

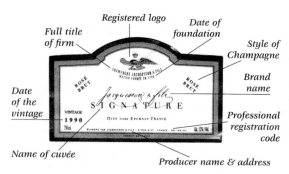

Registered logo · *Date of foundation* · *Full title of firm* · *Style of Champagne* · *Brand name* · *Date of the vintage* · *Professional registration code* · *Name of cuvée* · *Producer name & address*

Champagne bottle sizes

Champagne comes in ten bottle sizes. The bottles are made with heavy, thick glass; strong enough to contain the powerful pressure of the imprisoned fizz without breaking. Only the half bottle, bottle and magnum are sold without exception in the original vessel in which the second fermentation was conducted. The contents of the Jeroboam and larger sizes are transferred under pressure – a process called *transvasage* – from standard 750ml (26fl oz) bottles, as are those of quarter bottles. The vast bottle sizes, including the Salmanazar, Balthazar and Nebuchadnezzar, are making a modest comeback – perhaps with New Year's Eve 1999 on everyone's mind.

The different bottle sizes with their equivalent liquid volumes are as follows:

Quarter bottle	187ml (6·6fl oz)
Half bottle	375ml (13fl oz)
Bottle	750ml (26.4fl oz)
Magnum (two bottles)	1.5 litres (52.7fl oz)
Jeroboam (four bottles)	3 litres (105·6fl oz)
Rehoboam (six bottles)	4·5 litres (158fl oz)
Methuselah (eight bottles)	6 litres (211fl oz)
Salmanazar (12 bottles)	9 litres (317fl oz)
Balthazar (16 bottles)	12 litres (422fl oz)
Nebuchadnezzar (20 bottles)	20 litres (704fl oz)

Storing, opening and serving

For most readers who lack a real cellar beneath their house or apartment block, the most important point is to keep things simple. In choosing the best place to store Champagne, remember that it is like any other fine white wine.

The bottles should be stacked horizontally in as quiet and dark a spot as possible, since vibration and light are the enemies of fine wines while they are maturing. They should be kept well away from points of heat, somewhere where the temperature does not fluctuate too much. The range between 11–13°C (52–55°F) is ideal, but constancy of temperature is more important than coldness. It is therefore sensible to avoid areas like the kitchen, the garage and the garden shed. The floor of a lightly ventilated wardrobe in a cool dressing room or spare bedroom can make an excellent home for your precious fizz.

For the wealthy collector who has plenty of space, a prefabricated "cellar" can be installed in the home. There are two types: the electric temperature-controlled cabinet, which is specially designed to store all your wines, comes in various shapes and sizes, and can be plugged in anywhere. A more intriguing store, and certainly more expensive, is the "spiral staircase". This unit, which is made by Eurocave™, is a large steel cylinder with a spiral staircase. The bottles slot into spaces between the stairs. And a certain well-known French winewriter had one installed in the bathroom floor of his Paris apartment!

CHILL, NOT FREEZE

When cooling a Champagne it should be chilled, and not iced, as it is impossible to appreciate the flavour of a frozen wine which is opened at temperatures hovering above zero. The best and ideal temperature at which to serve Champagne is between 6–9°C (43–48°F).

Within this temperature range the bouquet and flavour of the Champagne are at their best, and the pressure of the fizz in the bottle is reduced to about one atmosphere. Consequently, this will minimise the risk of the wine gushing from the bottle (with the loss of precious fizz) when the cork is removed. Before serving a Champagne, put the bottle in the refrigerator (not the freezer) for about 100 minutes at a set temperature of 6°C (43°F).

If you are pushed for time to chill the Champagne, place the wine in an ice-bucket, which has been half-filled with ice and half with water, for 30 minutes. Inverting the bottle for the first ten minutes or so should ensure that all the wine is cooled evenly – if it has not been submerged, the top part of the bottle will be less cold than the main body so there is then the risk that the escaping fizz is more likely to froth over.

HOW TO OPEN THE BOTTLE

The theatrical "pop" as the cork is removed is part of the magic of Champagne, heralding a time to party. But if the bottle is expensive, it is better that the foaming bubbles be released quietly through the wine in the glass.

Here are a few ground rules to help you open the bottle with panache. Make sure that glasses are nearby – just in case. Cut off the foil around the cork; untwist and remove the wire muzzle. Place the chilled bottle on a flat surface. Hold the bottle in one hand, grasp the cork firmly in the other, with the thumb placed over the cork and the other fingers round the neck of the bottle.

Taking your time, ease the cork out of the bottle, teasing it backwards, forwards and upwards with your thumbs; or you can hold the bottle in one hand and turn and twist the cork with the other. As soon as the cork starts to give, tilt it away from your eyes and face (and those of your guests); at this point the palm of the hand should be used simultaneously to act as a brake to prevent the cork from shooting out of the bottle at high velocity.

When properly executed, the cork should emerge with a quiet sigh. Alternatively, specially designed Champagne tweezers can be used to extract the cork.

SERVING

Before serving Champagne (or any wine for that matter), pour a small amount into a glass, then smell it and taste it to ensure that there is no "corked" (ie musty or tainted) aromas or flavours.

During the 1990s, bad corks became far more common; the incidence is now reckoned to be unacceptable: one in twelve for most still wines and around one in twenty for sparkling wines. Be on your guard and, if you think you have a bad closure, stopper the wine with a Vacuvin™ or simple lever device and return it as soon as possible to the shop or store where you bought it, together with its cork. Be guided by the smell of the cork (and wine), not by its appearance. For example, after removal from the bottle, a Champagne cork normally expands to a mushroom shape, but sometimes it remains peg shaped – this can signal that the Champagne is out of condition, but not necessarily – it could simply indicate that the wine is old.

When pouring Champagne, the principle is to pour a tiny amount into each glass. Then, starting with the first glass, go back and top up each one. This is because the initial froth will have subsided by then, making it easier to fill the glasses – but ensure that they are no more than two-thirds full when served, for this allows the aromas of the Champagne to linger in the top of the glass and therefore be more fully appreciated.

GLASSES

Since glass blowing was first invented in the 17th century, there have been two types of glasses particularly associated with drinking Champagne.

The broad-topped *coupe*, created by Venetian glassmakers in the 1660s, became hugely popular in France from the time of the Belle Epoque until well into the current century. However, despite its *louche* associations, it is a poor glass in which to appreciate Champagne, as the lovingly produced bubbles go flat quickly and the wide brim allows much of the aroma to escape.

Nowadays the tall elongated flute is a more familiar Champagne glass. Elegant though it is, the flute still poses a problem, for its narrow cylindrical shape causes the wine to froth rapidly, making appreciation of its vinous flavours more difficult.

The ideal glass for both fine sparkling and still wines is the classic "tulip", with its bulbous base and inwardly tapering top, since it has the dual advantage of holding a decent amount of wine when just half full and of concentrating the wine's aromas in the upper half of the glass.

WASHING AND CLEANING

Never put good Champagne glasses in the dishwasher: quite apart from the danger of breakage, any trace of detergent left in the glass will leave a chemical smell, and can kill the wine's sparkle.

Always hand wash the glasses and rinse them thoroughly in hot (but not boiling) water, before drying and polishing them with a clean tea towel.

OPENED BOTTLES

Contrary to popular belief, the sparkle in Champagne need not disappear shortly after the wine has been opened. If the bottle is stoppered with a Vacuvin™ or simple lever device and returned to the refrigerator, the Champagne should keep its fizz for up to a week.

A good range of fancy, tailor-made Champagne-stoppers, designed for keeping partially consumed bottles, is available at most specialist wine shops.

Champagne and food

The marketing people involved with the big Champagne houses like to sell the idea that their wines go with almost any food (even game, meat and cheese). Properly aged vintage Champagnes do have the fullness, complexity and character to match most *cuisines*; but the younger, brisker non-vintage *cuvées* are more successful in the main when the dish is delicate and subtle.

There are several ranges of flavour combinations that are well worth trying. These all follow and are listed by style:

Bone-dry, sugarless Champagne (Extra, Ultra Brut)

A perfect match for oysters and other crustaceans, the acidity in the wine provides a fine and firm contrast to the soft, fat texture of the shellfish.

Very-dry, classic Champagne (Brut)

This style, particularly one of medium-weight examples from a great house such as Pol Roger or Billecart-Salmon, makes a good partner to a simply grilled or *sautéed* sole. A fuller-style Brut, such as Veuve Clicquot or Charles Heidsieck, might work better with sea bass or "sweet" scallops, while a Blanc de Noirs will suit something richer still, such as fish in a cream sauce.

A Champagne that has been fermented in wood – from Krug, Bollinger, Jacquesson or Selosse – has enough weight, flavour and vinosity to accompany white meats and subtler, lightly hung game birds such as partridge, woodcock and pigeon. It can also be an excellent match, and partner, for mature cheeses such as Gruyère and Tome de Savoie.

Rosé Champagne

A *rosé*, especially one with a high percentage of Pinot Noir, is a very adaptable wine and can complement a wide range of dishes.

It is excellent with charcuterie, *pâtés*, terrines and hams; and fairly matched with smoked fish. It can also prove interesting with spicy Asian *cuisine*, particularly crispy duck.

Medium-sweet Champagne (Demi-Sec)

This can be delicious with rich fruit cake (Christmas or wedding cake, for example), though I tend to find it less successful with fine desserts. And, like most wines, it usually fails as an accompaniment to chocolate.

Very sweet Champagne (Doux)

Really too unctuous to match desserts, but can be a pleasure on its own at the end of a meal as an alternative to port or Sauternes.

CHAMPAGNE IN COOKING

The wine of Champagne has been used as an ingredient in classic French *cuisine*, particularly sauce making, since the 18th century. In Menon's *Les Soupers de la Cour*, published in 1755, the wines of Champagne are listed as ingredients in a quarter of the 1,082 recipes for meats, poultry, terrines and sauces. Of course the wine was – and is – more important than just bubbles; clearly if you boil and reduce Champagne in a sauce, the froth disappears and contributes little to the quality of the dish. The still wine of Champagne, however, is ideal for cooking. Like a good Chablis or Riesling its acidity ensures that the sauce does not brown, and it adds freshness and delicacy of aroma to a white sauce in particular.

Still Champagne wine (Coteaux Champenois) can be an excellent base for braising mushrooms and truffles. On a less conventional note, a glass of sparkling Champagne added to barbecued fish at the last moment imparts something of its froth and delicacy to the dish.

Buying Champagne for the millennium

Of all the great wines of France, Champagne has a particular aptitude to mature and improve in bottle. The fact that it is seldom given the chance to do so is largely the fault of the large houses' sales policies; the result of Champagne being relentlessly presented as a wine for fêtes and celebration – to be drunk for immediate gratification as soon as it is put on the market. This is a pity because good Champagne needs ageing to soften the high levels of acidity that are the defining trait of its grapes, grown as they are in the cold climate of the 49th parallel.

The message for Champagne lovers is simple: think about your needs and buy the wine about a year before you plan to drink it. A case of non-vintage Champagne stored for a further 12 months in a cool corner of your house or apartment will pay dividends in terms of the mellowness of flavour it yields.

I recommend that you ignore the advice of disreputable wine-investment firms who claim that with the start of the third millennium on everyone's mind, there is likely to be a shortage of non-vintage Champagne in 1999, and a consequent rocketing of its prices. This is unlikely to happen. The stock levels in Champagne at the time of writing are very healthy, particularly of "blocked" wines from the '92, '93 and '94 vintages. These have all been wisely set aside by the Champagne authorities to allow for the possibility of an entire year's production (around 246 million bottles) being consumed on that particular New Year's Eve.

Vintage Champagnes are another matter. Like all fine wines, they are produced in limited quantities and now is the time to select those that will be *à point* on 31 December 1999. Generally, they are drunk far too young, as they rarely show their class before they are ten years old, and do not reach their peak until they reach their 13th, 15th, or even 20th birthdays.

The vintage of 1985 may come to be seen as one of the two greatest years in Champagne since the Second World War, the other being the '64. The '85s have exceptional concentration and fruitiness of flavour – the result of a small crop, and especially ripe Pinot Noir grapes. This particular vintage is fast disappearing from shop shelves, but by late 1998 and early 1999 specialist wine merchants should still have limited stocks of the greatest and inevitably most expensive wines, such as Krug and Bollinger.

The trio of '88, '89 and '90 constitute that rarity – a run of three excellent vintages in a row. Of the three, '88 is the most classic in the sense that it has a certain mineral austerity and the best capacity for ageing. The best '88s need to be kept until late 1999 to develop fully their aromas and flavours. The '89s are gloriously ripe and rich wines that have shown their open friendly character early, but will still hold well into the early 21st century.

The '90s have been lauded as the greatest wines of the trio, combining the ripeness of the '89s with the acid structure of the '88s. Personally, I am sceptical about the alleged greatness of '90 as a Champagne vintage. This was one of the hottest summers on record and the harvest was enormous, so it is not surprising that quality is variable, the less well made wines are lacking that "tension" essential to a great Champagne. They are also maturing much more quickly than was expected at the outset. The finest Champagnes from the '90s, however, are likely to be magnificent, combining an opulence of fruit with excellent acidity. They may be drunk with pleasure in 1999–2000, but are likely to be better still in 2003 and beyond.

Some of the smaller houses and growers will be offering their '93s (these are good, sound and clean Champagnes) in time for the millennium, and these could make pleasant drinking by then.

Other producers (especially the smallest growers) will also release their '95s at the same time. And while this is an excellent vintage – particularly for Chardonnay – it seems optimistic to believe that they will be ready to drink at just four years old.

A millennium selection

Highlighted below under various category headings are my suggestions of 37 Champagnes for drinking to celebrate the millennium. These particular wines have been chosen to give the broadest range of styles to suit all pockets:

Good-value buys in non-vintage Champagnes
Pierre Vaudon (Union Champagne); Waitrose Blanc de Noirs (Union Auboise); René Geoffroy Brut

Finest non-vintage Champagnes
Bollinger Special Cuvée; Billecart-Salmon Brut Réserve; Pol Roger White Foil; Veuve Clicquot Yellow Label; Pierre Gimmonet; Alain Robert Sélection (Blanc de Blancs)

Best non-vintage Rosé
Jacquesson Perfection Brut; R de Ruinart; Laurent-Perrier

Vintage/Prestige Selection
'85 Krug; Bollinger RD; Veuve Clicquot "La Grande Dame"; Salon Le Mesnil Blanc de Blancs
'88 Taittinger Comtes de Champagne; Jacquesson "Signature"; Pol Roger Cuvée Spéciale PR; Dom Ruinart Blanc de Blancs
'89 Jean-Mary Tarlant Cuvée Louis; Veuve Clicquot Brut Réserve; Louis Roederer Millésime; Bollinger Grande Année
'90 Daniel Dumont Brut Réserve; Pol Roger Vintage; Jacquesson "Signature" Rosé; Union Champagne Cuvée Orpale Blanc de Blancs; Alain Robert Le Mesnil; Duval-Leroy Cuvée des Roys; Dom Pérignon Brut and Rosé; Louis Roederer Cristal; Billecart-Salmon Grande Cuvée; Bruno Paillard; Joseph Perrier
'93 Jacquesson "Signature", René Geoffroy Cuvée Prestige

Directory of producers

Champagne

Outside France, the market for Champagne is generally dominated by the *grandes marques* – the great brands. This directory includes the wines of these 20 major firms in some detail, pointing the reader to those *cuvées* that are particularly worth seeking out and, occasionally, warning about those which I believe to be overrated.

Beyond the magic circle of the big names, Champagne offers a huge range of house styles. I have therefore focused particularly on 170 lesser-known producers, both sizeable cooperatives and smaller grower-Champagne-makers, who are likely to be the stars of tomorrow in Zurich, Frankfurt, Brussels, London and New York, where quality and value for money are the name of the game. The industry is in flux and "grower power" is likely to assert itself in Champagne in the first years of the 21st century, as it did in Burgundy during the 1980s.

The star-rating system and abbreviations used throughout this Directory of producers section are explained in the sections: How to use this book (*see* page 5) and Understanding the label (*see* page 20).

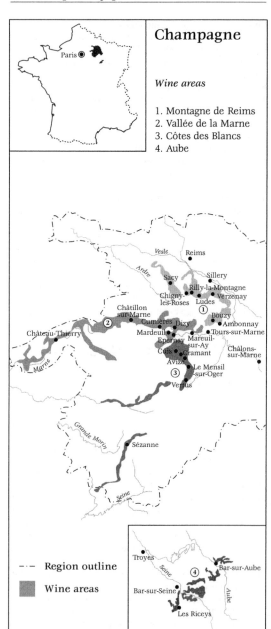

Champagne

Wine areas

1. Montagne de Reims
2. Vallée de la Marne
3. Côtes des Blancs
4. Aube

- - - Region outline

▓ Wine areas

Henri Abelé
NM 51500 Reims ☆☆

The third-oldest Champagne house (established 1757) with an interesting history. In 1884, *dégorgement à la glace*, the method of disgorging now used by all Champagne houses, was invented in the Henri Abelé cellars. It is currently owned by Freixenet, the giant Spanish cava producer.

Fine Chardonnay-led Champagnes, from the good Sourire de Reims NV to the exceptional prestige *cuvée*, Réserve du Repas, which is a Blanc de Blancs made only in exceptional years ('83, '85, '90).

Abel Lepitre
NM 51160 Mareuil-sur-Aÿ ☆

Founded in 1924 and greatly enlarged by Jacques Lepitre, son of the founder, after the Second World War. This house was famous in the 1960s for the excellence of its prestige *cuvée*, Prince A de Bourbon Parme. Since 1970, the firm has been a pawn in various takeovers by the big drinks groups and, having recently changed hands again, a question must hang over future quality.

However, during the early 1990s, the standard Brut NV was a well-aged, rounded Champagne dominated by Pinot Noir. The Réserve C Blanc de Blancs 1990 is an impeccable wine – fresh yet mellow and balanced.

Agrapart et fils
RM 51190 Avize ☆☆☆

The Agrapart family has been a grower-Champagne-maker for four generations and produces fine Blanc de Blancs of real purity of flavour, typical of Avize. The 1990 is a great success in this rich vintage – power and elegance in textbook harmony. Also, the Cuvée Spéciale Réserve Rosé NV is of exemplary finesse.

Jean-Antoine Ariston
RM 511170 Brouillet ☆☆

In the far northern valley of the Ardre, Jean-Antoine Ariston is a painstaking Champagne maker; growing all his own grapes, and buying in none. Finesse is the major virtue of both his Rosé de Noirs and vintage-dated Vieilles Vignes, which is dominated by Chardonnay.

Michel Arnould et fils
RM 51360 Verzenay ☆☆☆

This family of growers has been a reliable source of full, Pinot-led Champagnes since the 1960s. With Patrick Arnould now at the helm, the quality goes from strength to strength.

The Champagnes reflect the excellence of the grapes from his 12 hectares on the best slopes of Verzenay. The Brut NV is a true Blanc de Noirs – full and creamy Pinot Noir fruit that is in no way overblown. The Cuvée Signature 1990, which will be followed by the '93, is an impressive wine with a fine freshness, helped by the addition of 25-per-cent Chardonnay to the blend.

Aubry et fils
RM 51390 Jouey-les-Reims ☆☆

Remois growers since the French Revolution, the Aubry's farm 16 hectares of vines, and offer a compact range of Champagnes. The Pinot Meunier-led Brut Classique is aged in wood yet is very clean tasting, lively and persistent.

The vintage-dated Nicolas-François Aubry Sable Rosé is a classic *assemblage* of Pinot Noir and Chardonnay – pale in colour, but with enough complexity and vigour to match *sautéed* kidneys.

Autreau de Champillon
NM 51160 Champillon ☆☆

Although now trading as a *négociant*, the business is based on an old estate founded in the 1870s. Two recommended *cuvées*: the Réserve – a well-aged blend of black and white grapes, with fine toasty character; and the vintage-dated Les Perles de la Dhuy (great 1989) – fine evolved Chardonnay flavours.

Aube

– – – Region outline

Wine areas

Seine

● Bar-sur-Seine
│ Balnot-sur-
┆ Laignes ●
┆   ● Celles-sur-Ources

● Les Riceys

Avirey-Lingey ●

Ayala
NM 51160 Aÿ ☆☆

Rather out of fashion these days, this traditionalist house makes classic dry Champagnes that are good value for money. The Brut NV is pale-green-gold in colour, fresh and lemony and ages well. The vintage-dated Blanc de Blancs (very successful in '85 and '88) is usually a bargain.

Bagnost Père et fils
RM 51530 Pierry ☆☆

Claude Bagnost's family has owned this eight-hectare estate since 1912. Among the best *manipulants* in Pierry, Claude

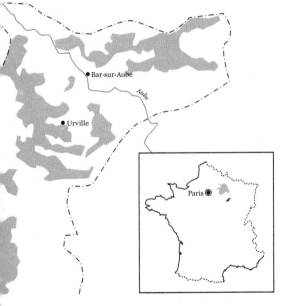

Bagnost shows a deft hand in blending the predominant Pinot Meunier with Chardonnay to produce a fine *rosé* Champagne – pale in colour, but with the fullness of flavour to match barbecued veal chops.

Christian Bannière
RM 51150 Bouzy ☆☆

A small grower in Bouzy, Christian Bannière is making ever-better Champagne from a few hectares of Grand Cru grapes.

The excellent Brut Tradition is virtually a Blanc de Noirs, with all the expansive generosity of great Pinot Noir (90 per cent), tempered with the freshness of Chardonnay. Only 15,000 bottles are made each year.

Paul Bara
RM 51150 Bouzy ☆☆☆

A prominent grower and Champagne maker who makes an exceptional Grand Rosé de Bouzy entirely from Pinot Noir – a sensuous Champagne redolent of raspberry- and strawberry-fruit flavours, and great with Thai and Cantonese dishes, especially spicy duck.

The vintage wines are fine expressions of generous, yet poised Pinot Noir. Note that the '89 will drink beautifully right up to 2000.

Barancourt
NM 51150 Bouzy ☆☆☆

Part of the Vranken group since 1994, a small merchant house established by three Bouzy growers in the mid-1960s specialising in Champagnes with a Pinot Noir content as high as 90 per cent.

Very good Cuvée des Fondateurs – displays rich, dense flavours, but is also aromatic and well balanced. And excellent Coteaux Champenois Rouge, especially the '90.

Bardoux Père et fils
RM 51390 Villedommange ☆☆

An old wine-growing family of the Petite Montagne de Reims, which started making its own Champagne in the late 1920s.

Pascal Bardoux's Brut typifies the attractive style of the Petite Montagne de Reims – fresh and floral, but well rounded with good length of flavour. In this *cuvée* the two Pinots account for 75 per cent of the blend. The 1990 vintage is rich and sensuous, with mature "animal" aromas.

Edmond Barnaut
RM 51150 Bouzy ☆☆☆

Another Bouzy grower who owns 15 hectares of highly rated vineyards. His most original *cuvée* is the Grande Réserve, which is based on a solera system.

In this procedure 50 per cent of the reserve wine is drawn off and replaced by the same quantity of new wine from the current vintage, so creating a reserve wine of increasing complexity. The result is an excellent Champagne – at once fine, floral, well structured and with real maturity of flavour.

Both the Sélection Extra Brut and the *rosé* are powerful Pinot-led blends, and are based on wines with an average age of seven years.

Baron Albert
NM 02310 Charly ☆☆

Growers turned merchants, the Barons own a 30-hectare vineyard at the western limit of the Champagne winefield (less than 50 miles from Paris). Their best wine is the vintage-dated Cuvée Jean de la Fontaine, named after the famous French fable writer who knew the vineyard. The Chardonnay-led 1989 is a rich, ripe wine for food.

Michel Baujean
RM 10340 Bagneux-la-Fosse ☆☆

A respected Aube grower, Michel Baujean makes a fine Brut Tradition from a classic mix of Pinot Noir and Chardonnay, with a *soupçon* of Pinot Meunier.

This is a wine of considerable class and refinement, showing a welcome new glimpse of the Aube's potential to make fine Champagne.

René Bauser
RM 10340 Les Riceys ☆☆☆

Founded in 1959, this 13-hectare *domaine*, sited around the best known communes of the southern Aube, is making a first-rate Blanc de Noirs with all the generous flavours of Les Riceys Pinot Noir. With impressive freshness and elegance, it offers very good value for money.

Herbert Beaufort
RM 51150 Bouzy ☆☆☆

An important Bouzy grower and Champagne maker who owns 15 hectares on the best hillsides of this area. The Carte d'Or Brut is almost a pure Blanc de Noirs, and is exuberantly fruity and intense.

This house, unusually for growers in Pinot Noir country, also makes an excellent Blanc de Blancs – the Cuvée du Melomane is fine yet ample, with a flattering touch of toast and vanilla.

Beaumet
NM 51207 Epernay ☆☆

Originally established in Pierry in 1878, Beaumet has been owned for 20 years by the Trouillard family. It is a medium-sized house, owning 30 hectares of Grand Cru vineyards in Avize, Cramant and Chouilly.

So, no surprise, by far the best wine produced here is the Cuvée Malakoff Blanc de Blancs, which is aged for a minimum of seven years. The standard Cuvée Brut is a classic *assemblage* of all three Champagne grapes – the resulting wine displays round, full and long flavours.

Beaumont des Crayères
CM 51530 Mardeuil ☆☆to☆☆☆

A small quality-conscious cooperative just west of Epernay, making pure, fruity Champagnes sold at keen prices. The Pinot Meunier-led Cuvée Réserve Brut is ideal for parties and weddings. The Cuvée Prestige is more powerful and complex.

Yves Beautrait
RM 51150 Louvois ☆☆☆

Lucky Yves Beautrait owns more than 16 hectares of Grand Cru vineyard, and the class of his grapes shines through in his Grand Cru Brut.

This is a blend of 75 per cent Pinot Noir and 25 per cent Chardonnay – a Champagne of sustained power, balanced by an exemplary finesse.

Billecart-Salmon
NM 51160 Mareuil-sur-Aÿ ☆☆☆☆

This house has always been a highly respected *grande marque*, and the small family firm is at the top of the tree for quality across the range.

It was Billecart-Salmon who pioneered the "cold settling" process, prior to the first fermentation, which ensures the freshness and long life in the finished Champagnes.

Their range of wines include a faultless Brut NV – vital yet honeyed, and subtle pale-coloured *rosé* which is Billecart-Salmon's flagship wine in the USA. There are also superb vintage wines and a magnificent late disgorged Grande Cuvée (especially '85).

H Blin & co
CM 51700 Vincelles ☆☆☆

In the heart of the Marne Valley, this cooperative of growers farms 112 hectares and shows just how delicious Pinot Meunier-based Champagne can be.

The Brut Tradition is made entirely from black grapes (90 per cent Pinot Meunier) – a ripe and golden wine, spicy, strong and mouthfilling. Also a fine, full *rosé*; and a first-rate, rich but fresh 1990 vintage with higher percentages of Pinot Noir and Chardonnay.

Thomas Blondel
NM 51500 Ludes ☆☆

This brand was launched in the mid-1980s, but the estate that provides most of the grapes for its *cuvées*, the Domaine des Monts-Forneaux, was established in the late 19th-century.

Very good, evolved *rosé* and fine-drawn Blanc de Blancs. Interesting older Chardonnay vintages, too.

Boizel
NM 51200 Epernay ☆☆☆

Since she took over the family business in 1984, the charming and straight-talking Evelyn Roques-Boizel has established a reputation for pure-flavoured Champagnes, faithful to their origins and very fairly priced.

To date, with the injection of capital from a consortium headed by Bruno Paillard, the Boizel label goes from strength to strength. The delicate and expressive Blanc de Blancs, and the delightful and exquisite ☆☆☆☆ 1988 Joyau de France are especially recommended.

Bollinger
NM 51160 Aÿ ☆☆☆☆

Founded in 1829 by Admiral de Villermont, an important landowner, and his future son-in-law Jacques Bollinger, a native of Württemberg. This famous Champagne house has a very traditionalist image; it certainly continues to make muscular Pinot Noir-dominated wine of body, depth, vinous complexity and exceptional longevity.

But, nothing stands still in the world of wine – even at Bollinger. For since Ghislain de Montgolfier, who is a direct descendant of the founder, took over the reins in 1995, the Bollinger style has changed very slightly, and in my view for the better. The Special Cuvée Brut, though still richly "Pinot", tastes cleaner and less oxidative than it used to. The delightfully expressive and elegant 1989 Grande Année has a touch more Chardonnay than usual (the 1990 has the legs to run a very long race).

The RD (recently disgorged) vintages continue to be aged *sur pointes* (neck down on the cork or cap) for optimal freshness, and for at least ten years (great 1985). Three tiny plots of ungrafted pre-*phylloxera* plots in Aÿ and Bouzy create the Vieilles Vignes Francaises – a rare and expensive wine, "combining the power of the New World, with the elegance of the old," in the words of Guy Bizot, the great nephew of the late Madame Lily Bollinger.

Alexandre Bonnet
NM 10340 Les Riceys ☆☆☆

A grower since the 18th century and a merchant since 1932, this Aube family firm tends its vines with meticulous care, as well as developing a thriving export business.

The vintage-dated Cuvée Madrigal is a sumptuous wine, a half Pinot Noir, half Chardonnay mix. Alexander Bonnet are also the main producer of the rare still Rosé des Riceys. Made on average only one year in three – in exceptional vintages like 1964, this wine can still taste good after 30 years in bottle.

Ferdinand Bonnet
NM 51055 Reims ☆☆

Founded in the 1920s at Oger on the Côte des Blancs, this little house was known for many years for its Chardonnay-led Champagnes.

It is now part of the Remy-Cointreau group and the wines are made in Reims alongside those of Charles Heidsieck and Piper-Heidsieck (qqv). Nowadays the *cuvées* have more black grapes than white in their composition, notably in the Brut

Heritage (with 50 per cent Pinot Meunier), which is plump, rounded and forward. Laytons Champagne, one of the best-value sparklers on the British market, is also made here.

Edmond Bonville
RM 51190 Oger ☆☆☆

This seven-hectare *domaine* makes a textbook example of the subtlety and refinement an Oger Champagne can attain.

Pure mature Chardonnay, of course, shapes the aromas of butter and walnuts in the excellent Blanc de Blancs Cuvée de Réserve – the palate is honeyed, yet fresh and long. A mini-Salon in the making!

Bouché Père et fils
NM 51530 Pierry ☆☆

This is a small independent house, founded after the Second World War, with a fine 35-hectare vineyard and plots in five Grands Crus. Good generously flavoured and naturally dry Brut NV; and the altogether excellent Cuvée Saphir, made from Grand Cru grapes in a blend of 60 per cent Pinot Noir, 40 per cent Chardonnay.

Raymond Boulard
NM 51480 La Neuville-aux-Larris ☆☆

An interesting smaller house, specialising in Champagnes dominated by black grapes, largely sourced from its own ten hectares of vineyards.

The Grand Cru Mailly (90 per cent Pinot Noir) is powerful yet balanced, and very typical of its provenance. A very good *rosé* of strawberry-like fruitiness, made from the two Pinots by the *saignée* method.

Bourgeois-Boulonnais
RM 51130 Vertus ☆☆

This house is a *récoltant-manipulant* with five hectares on the Côte des Blancs. They produce two good Chardonnay *cuvées* – a forward Blanc de Blancs, with a redolence of white peaches; and a tight-structured Grande Réserve, which is ideal (and should be) for longer keeping.

Château de Boursault
RM 51480 Boursault ☆☆

This is an impressive château, and holds commanding views over the Marne Valley. It was also once the country seat of the Widow Clicquot.

Today there is a nine-hectare vineyard which produces three creditable *cuvées* – a rich, deep-pink *rosé* made from the two Pinots; a vintage-dated Blanc de Blancs; and a fine prestige Tradition from a blend of 70 per cent Pinots Noir and Meunier and 30 per cent Chardonnay.

Boutillez-Guer
RM 51380 Villers-Marmery ☆☆

A grower on the Montagne de Reims since the middle ages, this family now makes its own Champagne.

The Chardonnay from Villers-Marmery is highly prized by the big houses for their blends. So, here is a chance to taste a grower's version, either as a supple Blanc de Blancs or as the main element (85 per cent) in the balanced and fine Cuvée Tradition.

Breton et fils
RM 51270 Congy ☆☆

A father and son duo. The Breton team makes a good incisive Blanc de Blancs; and a rich, rounded Brut dominated by Pinot Meunier from its five-hectare vineyard bordering the Marne Valley.

Brice
NM 51150 Bouzy ☆☆

A recent enterprise (1994) founded by two former directors of Barancourt Champagne (qv). The first tastings of these aromatic, clean, non-oxidative Champagnes – sourced from Premier Cru grapes – are promising.

Bricout
NM 51190 Avize ☆☆to☆☆☆

Founded in 1820 by Charles Koch's sons and Arthur Bricout, this Avize firm is associated with the *vedettes* of French showbusiness. Essentially a Chardonnay house, exemplified by the brilliant pure-flavoured Cuvée Prestige – elegant in its clear-glass bottle, with an exceptionally fine definition of Avize-based flavours.

The prestige *cuvée* Arthur Bricout is also Chardonnay dominated; the 1985 is still full of life and will reach its apogee in late 1999. The firm is now German owned.

Brochet-Hervieux
RM 51500 Ecueil ☆☆☆to☆☆☆☆

The Brochets, one of the oldest families of growers in the Marne Valley, farm 14 hectares of vines.

All the Champagnes in this cellar are immaculate, from the minimally dosed Pinot-led Extra Brut to the superb, voluptuous Cuvée Spéciale "HBH" 1990 – with aromas of fresh-grilled toast and flavours of super ripe orchard fruit. One of the greatest grower Champagnes from this rich year.

Jacky Broggini
NM 51500 Chigny les Roses ☆☆

A grower now with merchant status, Jacky Broggini makes a big, expansive Brut. The *cuvée* is dominated by Pinot Meunier

(75 per cent) – its succulent red-fruit flavours make it ideal to drink with a truffled *pâté en croûte* or roast guinea fowl.

Eric Bunel
RM 51150 Louvois ☆☆

Eric Bunel farms a seven-hectare Grand Cru vineyard at Louvois, planted with both Pinot Noir and Chardonnay. He makes a very good Brut – elegant, but structured, with a fine length of flavour.

Jacques Busin
RM 51630 Verzenay ☆☆☆

A *récoltant-manipulant* with eight hectares in the finest Grand Cru sites of Verzenay, Verzy, Ambonnay and Sillery.

The Carte d'Or NV shows all the *grandeur* and suppleness of great Pinot Noir (67 per cent), plus a fine note of evolving Chardonnay which makes up the remainder of the blend. Good quality-to-price ratio.

Pierre Callot
RM 51990 Avize ☆☆☆

Having been *vignerons* on the Côte des Blancs since the 1780s, the Callots have fine vineyards in Avize.

Their prize plot is half a hectare of very old vines, from which grapes are sourced for their splendid vintage-dated Vignes Anciennes Blanc de Blancs – a lees-aged, multi-flavoured wine of near-Burgundian complexity, to match richly sauced shellfish. Exceptional 1989.

Canard-Duchêne
NM 51500 Ludes ☆to☆☆

Although always modestly priced, the Brut NV unfortunately went through a bad patch in the early 1990s. However, under the reforming hand of *chef de caves* Jean-Jacques Lasalle, it is now fresher and cleaner.

The richly flavoured Cuvée Charles VII is a good buy, though all the Champagnes need more ageing in bottle. It is owned by Veuve Clicquot.

de Castellane
NM 51204 Epernay ☆☆to☆☆☆

Founded in 1895, this house close to the railway station is worth a visit – ascend the 400 steps to the top of the *grandiose* crenellated tower, visit the finely displayed Champagne museum, or stroll through the live butterfly garden in the summer months.

The standard Brut NV is briskly refreshing (if a bit young). Best wines are the characterful Blanc de Blancs NV and the excellent prestige vintage-dated Commodore – full and Pinot Noir-led. Superb 1989, reaching its apogee for the millennium.

Cattier
NM 51500 Chigny-les-Roses ☆☆

A grower on the Montagne de Reims since the 18th century; the Cattiers became a merchant in 1920.

A small quality-conscious firm with a good range of refined Champagnes, typified by the elegant Premier Cru and the supple, aromatic Clos du Moulin from the family's own 2.2-hectare walled vineyard.

Claude Cazals
RM 51190 Le Mesnil-sur-Oger ☆☆

A respected Le Mesnil grower and Champagne maker with nearly nine hectares in Grand Cru and Premier Cru sites on the Côte des Blancs.

The Extra Brut (minimally dosed) is a typical Le Mesnil *monocru* Champagne of good maturity, with punchy evolved Chardonnay flavours and notes of butter and almonds.

Charles de Cazanove
NM 51200 Epernay ☆☆

A traditionalist Chardonnay house founded at Avize in 1811. Currently owned by the Lombard family, which has lavished a lot of money on new equipment since 1985.

Also, both the Brut Azur and the Stradivarius Tête de Cuvée (exceptional 1989) are Chardonnay-led Champagnes, and are of real finesse.

Chanoine
NM 51100 Reims ☆☆

One of the oldest Champagne houses (1730), now making a range of incisive well-made wines at reasonable prices.

Earmark the Grande Réserve, a classic *assemblage* of all three Champagne grapes in equal proportions – well aged and rounded, with a fine definition of red-fruits flavours.

Chapuy
NM 51190 Oger ☆☆

An Oger grower and merchant with a six-hectare vineyard, Chapuy makes a range of sound Blanc de Blancs and an attractive Chardonnay-led Rosé. His standard Brut is an interesting mix of 75 per cent Chardonnay and 25 per cent Pinot Meunier.

Charbaut et fils
NM 51200 Epernay ☆

The future *cuvées* of this house may be subject to change following its purchase by the acquisitive Vranken group.

To date, the best wine has been the vintage-dated Blanc de Blancs Certificate – the fine 1988 had a well-judged autolytic character without loss of balance and fruitiness.

Guy Charlemagne
RM 51190 Le Mesnil-sur-Oger ☆☆☆

An aptly named grower in arguably the greatest village of the Côte des Blancs, making Champagnes of rare vinosity, depth and complexity. His Blanc de Blancs Mesnilésimé (great 1990) has enough presence to partner as richly flavoured food as sauced lobster or *foie gras*.

A Chauvet
NM 51150 Tours-sur-Marne ☆☆☆

This small family merchant business, owning 12 hectares of vines in the best sites, deserves to be better known.

Champagnes of personality, savour and style across the range. From the mouthfilling Brut, through the fruit-laden Grand Rosé to the very classy Blanc de Blancs Cachet Vert (a blend of three vintages, none less than seven years old).

Richard Cheurlin
RM 10110 Celles-sur-Ource ☆☆☆

Starting in 1978, Richard Cheurlin in 20 years has established himself as one of the best grower-Champagne-makers of the Aube. From seven hectares of vines, he makes three *cuvées* – Brut H, Carte d'Or and vintage-dated Cuvée Jeanne (1991). Each Champagne displays deftly blended flavours of ripe and rich Pinot Noir and racy, lemon-toned Chardonnay. All are excellent.

Gaston Chiquet
RM 51150 Dizy ☆☆

Established *récoltant* making interesting Champagnes, allying power and structure to fragrance and finesse. Excellent Spéciale Club 1990 – dominated by Chardonnay.

Veuve Clicquot-Ponsardin
NM 51100 Reims ☆☆☆☆

Of all the great brands of Champagne, "The Widow" is currently the most impressive. Over nine million bottles are produced every year, yet the quality and style – rich, full-bodied, beautifully balanced – never falters. Jacques Peters, the *chef de caves*, leads a very strong team responsible for the extraordinarily consistent Yellow Label NV, one of Champagne's surest things.

The most original wine is the vintage-dated Rich Réserve, with a *dosage* of 26 grams of sugar per litre. Neither really sweet nor classically dry, it is a brilliant partner for Asiatic *cuisine*. The prestige La Grande Dame is a masterpiece of mouth-enveloping richness (superb 1985), and La Grande Dame Rosé 1988 – only first released in 1996 has been lauded a fine pink Champagne. The current straight vintage, the 1990, is a beautiful, close-knit wine destined for a long life.

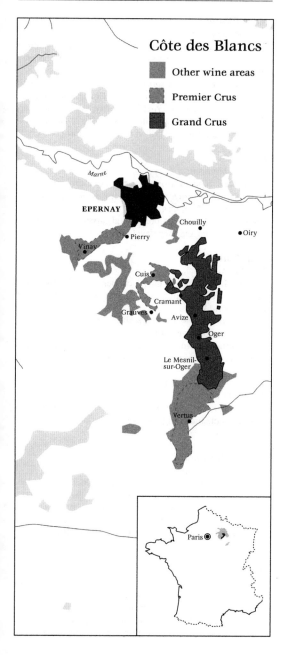

Côte des Blancs

- Other wine areas
- Premier Crus
- Grand Crus

Marne

EPERNAY

Chouilly

● Oiry

● Pierry

Vinay

Cuis ●

Cramant
Grauves ●
Avize ●

Oger ●

Le Mesnil-
sur-Oger

Vertus ●

Paris ●

André Clouet
RM 51150 Bouzy ☆☆☆

Pierre and Françoise Santz-Clouet run this nine-hectare estate on some of the best slopes of Bouzy and Ambonnay with exemplary care.

Its wines are the best sort of grower's Champagnes, with a vivid taste of their origins. The Grand Cru Brut Réserve is a big rich Pinot Noir wine typical of Bouzy; and the heather-coloured *rosé* brims with primary strawberry-like fruit, a Champagne to drink with grilled fish or Beaufort cheese.

Cocteaux
RM 51260 Montgenost ☆☆

On the back road to Troyes, at the southern end of the Sézannais, lies Montgenost, a sleepy little wine village producing rustic Champagnes.

Michel Cocteaux's Chardonnay-led *cuvées* are a cut above the rest – delicate and long flavoured.

Raoul Collet
CM 51160 Aÿ ☆☆

This is the brand name of the Aÿ cooperative, which was one of the first grower-groupings to be established at the end of the First World War.

Typical of an Aÿ-based *cuvée*, the Carte Noir is a blend of 75 per cent Pinot Noir, 24 per cent Chardonnay, 1 per cent Pinot Meunier – a sturdy Champagne of power and vinosity. The cooperative also produces a vintage-dated Carte d'Or.

Comte A de Dampierre
NM 51140 Chenay ☆☆

A bijou merchant specialising in costly *cuvées* at the top end of the market, including a superb Blanc de Blancs Cuvée Prestige 1985.

Jacques Defrance
RM 10340 Les Riceys ☆☆☆

A leading producer of the rare Rosé des Riceys; the 1990, tasted in 1997, is exceptional and could well live for 30 years.

The Defrance family also makes a good, full, Pinot Noir-dominated Brut Champagne, and even a fine Blanc de Blancs (an unlooked for boon in this home of great Pinot)!

Dehours
NM 51700 Cerseuil ☆☆

Owned by the Dehours family themselves, this is a small merchant house, and makes the admired "Confidentielle de Dehours" *cuvée*. An *assemblage* of 70 per cent Pinot Noir, 30 per cent Chardonnay; it is a fine and complex Champagne, striking a good balance between power and finesse.

Delamotte Père et fils

NM 51190 Le Mesnil-sur-Oger ☆☆☆

A very old Reims house (1760), long associated with Lanson. Now based in Le Mesnil and managed in tandem with Salon by Laurent-Perrier (qqv).

Chardonnay grapes dominate the blends: a stylish Brut NV – apricot scented, round yet fine, forward and ripe Blancs de Blancs 1990. Plus the impressive prestige Nicolas Louis Delamotte, largely sourced from top-rated Le Mesnil grapes.

André Delaunois

RM 51500 Rilly-la-Montagne ☆☆☆

A *récoltant-manipulant* with eight hectares of Premier Cru vineyards, using a high proportion of Rilly Chardonnay in his Champagnes. Most notably in his much admired Cuvée du Fondateur – a succulent and evolved wine, with complex secondary flavours.

Delbeck

NM 51053 Reims ☆☆

Founded in 1832, Delbeck was the favourite Champagne of the Citizen-King, Louis Philippe. Unfortunately the brand disappeared for 30 years until the 1960s, when it was resuscitated by François d'Aulan.

A Pinot Noir-based house, best in vintage Champagnes – the 1985 was a great structured wine; the 1990 is rounder and more forward.

Demoiselle

NM 51200 Epernay ☆

The "fighting brand" of the dynamic Vranken group. Light *apéritif* style, based on Chardonnay grapes – decent quality, though young tasting.

Paul Dethune

RM 51150 Ambonnay ☆☆☆

Paul Dethune has seven hectares on the best Ambonnay hillsides, from which he produces a very fine Pinot-led Grand Cru Brut with all the harmony of full flavours that makes Ambonnay such a highly regarded *cru*.

The *rosé* is excellent too – salmon pink in colour, it has a rich "Noir" flavour, proudly balanced by the incisive flavour of top-flight Chardonnay.

Deutz

NM 51160 Aÿ ☆☆☆☆

Formerly a proud family business with a justified reputation in the Champagne business for wines of the highest class. It is now owned and managed by Louis Roederer (qv), which is pouring money into the renovation of the house and cellars.

The Roederer touch shows to good effect in the classic Brut – creamy, yet decidedly dry in the true Deutz tradition. The vintage-dated Blanc de Blancs (especially the 1989) is a majestic wine for food; the prestige William Deutz is a superb wine of great vinous subtlety (lovely 1988).

De Venoge
NM 51204 Epernay ☆☆
This is a reasonably sized merchant house, which is now owned by the Remy Martin group. It produces pleasant, soft and supple Champagnes. And very good vintage Blanc de Blancs.

Pierre Domi
RM 51190 Grauves ☆☆
This is a Grauves estate, extending over eight hectares, and founded after the Second World War. A very good Grande Réserve shows what can be done when the dominant Pinot Meunier is blended with fine Chardonnay – soft and spicy, but refreshing and vital.

Doquet-Jeanmaire
NM 51130 Vertus ☆☆☆
Doquet-Jeanmaire is a small Vertus merchant-grower with 14 hectares of vineyards, including some especially fine sites in Le Mesnil-sur-Oger.

There are two exceptional wines: the vintage-dated Blanc de Blancs is beautifully made and crafted to retain its freshness for a good ten to fifteen years (very fine in 1995 and 1989, both great Chardonnay years); and the prestige Coeur de Terroir, also a pure Chardonnay but with a higher percentage of top Mesnil grapes in the blend.

Etienne Doue
RM 10300 Montgueux ☆☆☆
On the great south-facing hill of Montgueux, to the west of Troyes, Etienne Doue grows excellent, very ripe Chardonnay grapes which are the motor of his Grande Réserve and the predominant variety in his well-aged Sélection – a blend of three years.

This is a voluptuous style of Champagne with the flavours of Mediterranean fruits. Great value.

Robert Doyard et Fils
RM 51130 Vertus ☆☆
This family has been making its own Champagne from a six-hectare vineyard since the 1920s.

The current generation can be relied upon to produce vital and incisive Chardonnay flavours, especially in the Blanc de Blancs Brut Réserve.

Drappier
NM 10200 Urville ☆☆☆

From a long line of growers in the Bar-sur-Aube region, "Papa Pinot" Drappier was the first one to replace the Gamay grape with Pinot Noir at Urville in the 1930s. Nowadays this is a dynamic merchant-grower house, making hedonistic Champagnes of great character.

The heart of the business is the 38-hectare Urville *domaine*, the source of the beautiful Pinot Noir grapes used in the blends. All the wines are immaculate: the red-fruits-flavoured Carte d'Or Brut; a vinous bone-dry Brut Zéro; and the magnificent Grande Sendrée, whose very Pinot Noir character is tempered by the right amount of Chardonnay.

Claude Dubois
RM 51480 Venteuil ☆☆

This grower, stationed in the Marne Valley, is known for his Cuvée Le Rédempteur – a wood-aged Blanc de Noirs which is dominated by Pinot Meunier. This is a rich and mouthfilling Champagne for the table, and an especially good partner for lightly hung game.

Robert Dufour et fils
RM 10110 Landreville ☆☆

A gifted Aube grower and Champagne maker, Robert Dufour is a fine exponent of Chardonnay-influenced wines in an area better known for Pinot Noir.

A well-balanced Brut (half Pinot Noir, half Chardonnay) and a successful vintage-date Cuvée Prestige, with not a single black grape in the *assemblage*.

Dumenil
RM 51500 Chigny-les-Roses ☆☆

Long-established growers at Chigny, the Dumenils make good Champagnes typical of this Premier Cru on the Montagne de Reims. The Brut is rounded but fresh; the *rosé* redolent of orchard fruits; and the vintage often matures early, but with the structure to last well in bottle.

Daniel Dumont
RM 51500 Rilly-la-Montagne ☆☆☆

Growers and nurserymen cultivating 200,000 vines a year for sale to other producers. First-rate Champagnes, especially the well-aged Grande Réserve and the very fine Demi-Sec.

Duval-Leroy
NM 51130 Vertus ☆☆☆

Always a fine Champagne house, well-known to shrewd British wine shippers as the source of excellent wines at keen prices (usually sold under Buyer's Own Brand labels).

Under the direction of Carol Duval, the firm's current strategy is now to establish the Duval-Leroy brand on world markets. Its strong cards are 138 hectares of top-flight vineyards in the Côte des Blancs.

The excellent Chardonnay-led Fleur de Champagne; fine vintage-dated Blanc de Blancs (especially the 1990); and a durably structured prestige Cuvée des Roys are exceptional value for money.

Egly-Ouriet
RM 51150 Ambonnay ☆☆☆
Excellent *récoltants-manipulants* who make full and rich styles from seven hectares of Grand Cru grapes.

Three recommended *cuvées* include the mouthfilling Pinot-dominated Brut Tradition; the powerful Blancs de Noirs (a good wine with veal and white meats); and the vinous Vieilles Vignes.

Charles Ellner
NM 51207 Epernay ☆☆
Growers since the beginning of the century, the Ellners became merchants in the 1970s. The family's important vineyard of 54 hectares, in 15 communes, provides most of their grape needs.

The very good Qualité Extra, dominated by Pinot Noir, has an average age of six years on lees. Fine older vintages.

M Ferat et fils
RM 51330 Vertus ☆☆☆
A rising star among the Blanc de Blancs producers, Pascal Ferat cultivates ten hectares of Premier Cru vineyards.

His Chardonnay Champagne is everything one should be: incisive, clean as a whistle, with great purity of fruit and aptitude to age beautifully. The toasty, hazelnut-scented 1990 is lovely.

Nicolas Feuillatte
CM 51206 Chouilly ☆☆
Top Premier Cru Champagnes from the Centre Vinicole de la Champagne (CVC) – the region's biggest cooperative.

Quality across the range is sound, with the occasional superb bottle. Earmark the Palmes d'Or 1990, a true ☆☆☆☆ Chardonnay-led classic – fresh, vital yet honeyed; also the Cuvée Spéciale 1988 – mineral-rich and complex.

Roland Fliniaux
NM 51160 Aÿ ☆☆
A very small traditional grower-merchant business run by Régis Fliniaux. The grapes come from the three hectares of family holdings of Grand Cru Pinot Noir in Aÿ, and from

other growers in the commune. These are a full-bodied, old-fashioned "Noir" style of Champagne, and culminate in a splendid gutsy *rosé*.

Fleury
NM 10250 Courtezon ☆☆☆

Biodynamic viticulture and J-P Fleury's talent result in an exciting range of pure-flavoured Pinot Noir Champagnes. Brilliant *saignée rosé* and a very fine 1988 vintage, as good as any in the Aube.

Guy de Forez
RM 10340 Les Riceys ☆☆

A newcomer in the Barsequenais, Guy de Forez offers a well-made Brut, dominated by Pinot Noir. He also makes a very good still Rosé des Riceys (the 1990 is especially good).

Fresnet-Juillet
RM 51380 Verzy ☆☆☆

A fine domaine of nine hectares with holdings in Verzy, Mailly and Bisseuil. The Premier Cru Brut is a beautifully balanced Champagne whose subtle floral aroma belies its high Pinot Noir content of 80 per cent.

Also recommended is the Chardonnay-led, vintage-dated Special Club.

Gaidoz-Forget
RM 51500 Ludes ☆☆☆

A leading Ludes *domaine,* currently on top form. Gaidoz-Forget is greatly admired for its superb deep-flavoured *rosé* made from both Pinots (the Meunier is dominant).

A very fine Cuvée de Réserve, again black grapes led, has an average age of eight years on lees – maturity and freshness in perfect balance.

Gallimard Père et fils
RM 10340 Les Riceys ☆☆☆

A top-flight Barsequenais grower, offering an outstanding and voluptuous *rosé* Champagne. This is an ideal food wine and is redolent of orchard fruits.

It also produces good, textbook examples of potentially long-lived still Rosé des Riceys (especially 1988, 1990).

Georges Gardet
NM 51500 Chigny-les-Roses ☆☆to☆☆☆

This house produces rich and well-aged Champagnes, which are made mainly with highly rated Pinot Noir grapes from the Montagne de Reims.

All the Champagnes carry a date of disgorging. They are popular in the UK and have a second label, Boucheron.

Gatinois
RM 51160 Aÿ ☆☆☆
Small *récoltant-manipulant* making structured Pinot Noir-based Champagne and still-red Coteaux Champenois in great years (1989, 1990). High quality.

Gauthier
NM 51200 Epernay ☆☆
One of the better labels from the anonymous, but giant, house Marne et Champagne. Good, sound Grande Réserve – a classic blend with a slight majority of Chardonnay. Well-priced vintages (fine 1988).

René Geoffroy
RM 51480 Cumières ☆☆☆
Family members have been *vignerons* in the Marne Valley since the 16th century, with excellent Premier Cru holdings.

Undoubtably the best sort of traditional producers, using part-fermentation in wood and late disgorging of vintage Champagnes. First-rate, rich Cuvée Prestige 1990 and a fine, elegant 1993. Also an excellent Cumières Rouge.

Henri Germain
NM 51500 Rilly-la-Montagne ☆☆
Founded at the end of the 19th century and now part of the Frey group, Germain's 40-hectare vineyard provides about 40 per cent of its grape needs.

Thoroughly decent, full and well-rounded Champagnes, though still young to taste. Blanc de Noirs and the Belle de Germain *rosé* are recommended.

Pierre Gimmonet et fils
RM 51530 Cuis ☆☆☆
They have been Cuis growers since the 18th century, now with enviably fine holdings on the Côte des Blancs, including old vines in the best part of Cramant. The meticulous winemaking, and long-ageing *sur-pointes,* shape an elegant and subtle style of wine.

The wines include the brilliant, bone-dry Maxi-Brut; and the racy Cuvée Gastronome is all finesse. They are both perfect with oysters.

Paul Goerg
CM 51130 Vertus ☆☆
The brand name of the respected Coopérative Agricole et Vinicole "La Goutte d'Or", the grapes are sourced from 130 hectares of great Chardonnay sites in Le Mesnil, Vertus and Bergeres-les-Vertus.

Note that the exemplary and long-flavoured Blanc de Blancs is a great buy.

Michel Gonet et fils

RM 51190 Avize ☆☆

An important grower with 40 hectares of Chardonnay vines. Specialises in *apéritif* style Blanc de Blancs for early drinking. Sound quality.

Gosset

NM 51160 Aÿ ☆☆to☆☆☆

The Gossets had been making wine in Aÿ since the late 16th-century, so they could rightly claim to be the oldest house in the Marne Valley. After 400 years of family ownership, control of the firm passed in 1994 to another traditionalist, Max Cointreau of Frapin Cognac.

The new Brut Excellence is a sprightly Chardonnay-led Champagne, though by far the best *cuvées* here are the rich and multi-flavoured Grande Réserve and the sensuous, deeply flavoured Grand Millésime Rosé. The older vintage Champagnes have a mixed reputation – one either loves or hates their distinctive oxidative style.

George Goulet

NM 51100 Reims ☆☆

Popular in the UK before the Second World War, and a personal favourite of George VI, this low-key Reims house still makes fine Champagnes.

Classy Chardonnay-dominated Brut NV; a complex *rosé* and long-lived vintage Champagnes, such as the impressively fresh-tasting 1989. Underrated.

Henri Goutorbe

RM 51160 Aÿ ☆☆☆

The Goutorbes are both vine nurserymen and Champagne makers, owning 20 hectares of Grand Cru vineyards at Aÿ.

Full and rich Champagnes dominated by Pinot Noir, but well balanced, with great purity of flavour. A poised and structured Cuvée Prestige; an excellent *rosé*; and fine old vintages under the Millésime Rare label.

Alfred Gratien

NM 51201 Epernay ☆☆☆

They have rigorously old-fashioned winemaking methods, including fermentation in wood, which results in one of the most distinctive styles of Champagne.

The Brut NV has an unmistakable scent of fresh-baked bread, typical of its high Pinot Meunier content. The vintage wines are Chardonnay driven, and very long-lived due to avoidance of the malolactic fermentation. The magnificent prestige *cuvée* Paradis is super refined yet exotic, and is made from an unusual mix of 70 per cent Chardonnay and 30 per cent Pinot Meunier.

J M Gremillet
RM 10340 Balnot-sur-Laignes ☆☆

This is a serious grower based in the Aube region, who makes concentrated Champagnes from low-yielding Pinot Noir and Chardonnay vines. The vintage Blanc de Blancs Champagne is especially good.

Emille Hamm
NM 51160 Aÿ ☆☆

A family of Alsatian origin who became Champagne growers and merchants in Aÿ, producing pure, very dry Champagnes (with less than one per cent *dosage*). The fine Premier Cru Réserve is a bargain.

Charles Heidsieck
NM 51066 Reims ☆☆☆☆

Always a prestigious *grande marque*, this house has gone from strength to strength since 1985, when Daniel Thibault, an inspired winemaker, was appointed as *chef de caves*.

Of the range: the outstanding quality of the Brut Réserve owes everything to natural, non-interventionist vinification and to the complexity of the blend, which includes 300 different components. With 40 per cent *réserve* wines, this is a sumptuous and refined Champagne and structured to be enjoyed with fine *cuisine*.

The other great Thibault creation is the vintage-dated Blanc des Millénaires (superb 1985), one of the greatest and least austere Blancs de Blancs. The straight 1990 vintage is also among the finest of Champagnes.

Heidsieck Monopole
NM 51200 Epernay ☆☆

This old and famous, but unfortunately ailing, *grande marque* was acquired in 1996 by the Vranken group. Under the new *régime*, the Brut Dry Blue Label is better, fresher and cleaner tasting than previously.

A bottle of the prestige Diamant Bleu 1985, which I tasted in 1997, was excellent – a full-bodied, Pinot-led Champagne, approaching its apogee.

Piper-Heidsieck
NM 51066 Reims ☆☆

Sharing a beautiful new winery on the outskirts of Reims with its sister house Charles Heidsieck (qv), Piper-Heidsieck has benefited greatly from the Thibault touch since 1989.

Previously the range of Champagnes has been austere and reductive, they now have more fruit and charm. The easy, early drinking *rosé* is delightful; the prestige vintage Champagne Rare a great classic wine of exemplary finesse – well priced too.

Henriet-Bazin
RM 51380 Villers-Marmery ☆☆

A *récoltant-manipulant* with six hectares, Henriet Bazin makes a very good Premier Cru Brut entirely from Chardonnay.

The great white grape also shares an equal billing with Pinot Noir in the Premier Cru Sélection – a richer and more rounded wine for food.

Henriot
NM 51066 Reims ☆☆*to*☆☆☆

Having been growers in Champagne since the 17th century, and merchants since 1808, the Henriots owned 110 hectares of superb vineyards, mainly on the Côte des Blancs, unitl 1994. That year Joseph Henriot took the firm back from the LVMH group, but the price of independence was the loss of title to these assets.

Nevertheless, the Champagnes are still made from high-class Chardonnay and Pinot Noir (no Pinot Meunier is used). The Brut Souverain is a big beefy Champagne (not to my taste); the Blanc de Blancs NV is incisively excellent; and the prestige *cuvée* Enchanteleurs is very long-lived (the 1985 will be a point in late 1999).

M Hostomme et fils
NM 51530 Chouilly ☆☆*to*☆☆☆

A good producer of predominantly Chardonnay-based Champagnes. These include a mouthfilling, yet balanced Blanc de Blancs NV; and a fine evolved vintage Cuvée Harmonie, which is made from a blend of 70 per cent Chardonnay and 30 per cent Pinot Noir and only released after 6 years on lees.

J-P Husson
NM 51160 Aÿ ☆☆☆

The Hussons have recently acquired merchant status, but they remain close to the soil, for essentially they are nurserymen and growers.

With a five-hectare vineyard, they make classic Aÿ-based Champagnes which are full of ample Pinot flavours. An excellent bone-dry Brut Integral (tiny *dosage*) and Coteaux Champenois Rouge.

Robert Jacob
RM 10110 Merrey-sur-Arce ☆☆

Starting in the 1970s, Robert Jacob now farms 13 hectares in the Barsequenais. Yet another case of a fine Chardonnay Champagne, sourced in the region of Pinot Noir.

The 1990 Prestige (a Blanc de Blancs) displays exemplary freshness and attack, a pleasant change from too many unctuous wines from this very ripe year.

Jacquart
NM 51100 Reims ☆☆*to*☆☆☆

Now the sixth largest Champagne house – a cooperative turned merchant, deriving its strength from 1,000 hectares of vines owned by its members.

Clean, well-balanced Brut Tradition NV; classy citrus-like Brut Selection; racy vintages (excellent 1990) and refined prestige *cuvée* Nominée Blanc de Blancs.

André Jacquart et fils
RM 51190 Le Mesnil-sur-Oger ☆☆☆

Leading Mesnil growers with 11 hectares on the Côte des Blancs, and smaller holdings of black grapes in the Marne Valley and the Aube.

The Carte Blanche Brut is one of the best and most fairly priced NV Champagnes on the market, the flavour of top-flight Chardonnays rounded out with the richer taste of early maturing Pinot Noir. Also, a fine vintage Blanc de Blanc (excellent honeyed and fresh 1990).

Jacquesson
NM 51530 Dizy ☆☆☆☆

Founded in 1798 and one of the most important Champagne houses in the mid-19th-century.

Jacquesson is nowadays a small concern devoted to the highest standards of classical Champagne making. Run by the passionate Chiquet brothers, the firm offers the excellent Perfection Brut NV in white and *rosé* – both supple, creamy Champagnes of real vinosity.

The magnificent vintage-dated Blanc de Blancs is a pure Avize, while the 100-per-cent wood-fermented Signature prestige *cuvées* are great wines of multi-layered complexity. Kind prices for the quality offered.

René Jardin
RM 51190 Le Mesnil-sur-Oger ☆☆*to*☆☆☆

The Jardins have deep roots in Le Mesnil and now own 15 hectares in excellent hillside sites of the Côte des Blancs.

The Blanc de Blancs Cuvée Louis René has great breed and subtlety, showing the unerring class of Le Mesnil grapes at their best.

Jeanmaire
NM 51207 Epernay ☆☆

Founded in the 1930s and now owned by the Trouillard family, Jeanmaire is a good source of reliable Champagnes in a floral and clean style.

Well-balanced Brut NV – a classic blend of the three Champagne grapes, and an attractive vintage-dated Blanc de Blancs – fresh yet ripely mature.

Krug
NM 51100 Reims ☆☆☆☆

The most prestigious name in Champagne and ruinously priced. However, the wines are unique, with a style quite unlike any other.

Krug is the only house to ferment all of its wines in small oak barriques – which shape the full, rich, ultra-complex house style. But, the real quality factor in the superlative Grande Cuvée is the intricacy of the blend. This is composed each year by the fifth and sixth generations of the family, and it could include between 40 and 50 wines from 10 to 12 different vintages.

The vintage wines are very long lived, especially the single-vineyard Clos du Mesnil (the 1985 will mature well into the 21st century). The Krug Rosé is a masterpiece – delightfully fruity yet emphatically dry, this wine was once the centrepiece of an entire meal devised by the great Parisian chef, Alain Senderens.

Lacroix
RM 51700 Montigny-sur-Châtillon ☆☆☆

Top-flight growers in the Marne Valley, the Lacroix family planted their vineyard in the 1950s and launched their first Champagne brand in the 1970s.

These are Champagnes of body, structure and presence, dominated by black grapes. The Brut Tradition (70 per cent Pinot Meunier) is a big, golden wine, a third of the grapes for which were wood fermented. Excellent *rosé* and long-flavoured Grande Réserve.

Charles Lafitte
NM 51150 Tours-sur-Marne ☆☆

This house is a superior brand of the Vranken group. Both the half-and-half-black-and-white grapes Brut NV blend and the 100-per-cent-Chardonnay Grand Prestige are recommended for their finesse and balance.

Lanson
NM 51056 Reims ☆☆☆

The future looked black in 1991 when Lanson – one of the grandest of the *grandes maisons* – lost all 208 hectares of its superb vineyards as part of the terms of sale to the giant company, Marne et Champagne. But the new owners have confounded the critics, for the quality of the entire range at the end of the 1990s is immaculate.

The range extends from the powerful Pinot-led Black Label to the aromatic, well-aged *rosé*; through the broad-shouldered, deep-flavoured vintages (excellent 1989) to one of the longest-lived Champagnes – the supremely elegant, Chardonnay-rich Noble Cuvée.

Larmandier-Bernier
RM 51130 Vertus ☆☆☆

Combining 11 hectares of excellent Chardonnay sites on the Côte des Blancs, with Pierre Larmandier's own talent for winemaking, Larmandier-Bernier produces some of the most pure-flavoured and stylish Blanc de Blancs. Exceptional Cramant Grand Cru (1990, 1992).

Lassaigne-Berlot
RM 10150 Montgueux ☆☆☆

A leading grower, Christian Lassaigne makes excellent own-label, ripe, Chardonnay-based Champagnes. First-rate Cuvée Scintillante.

Raymond Laurent
RM 10110 Celles-sur-Ource ☆☆☆

One of the great characters of the Aube, Raymond Laurent bears a striking resemblance to Bismarck. His specialities are older vintages of Blancs de Noirs back to 1976 – Champagnes as warmly characterful as their maker.

Laurenti
RM 10340 Les Riceys ☆☆

Papa Laurenti and sons, Dominique and Bruno, run this 14-hectare vineyard, planted with 90 per cent Pinot Noir and 10 per cent Chardonnay.

The Brut Grande Cuvée, both white and *rosé*, are full of red-fruit flavours.

Laurent-Perrier
51150 Tours-sur-Marne ☆☆☆

Here, a great independent Champagne house and essentially the achievement of Bernard de Nonancourt after the Second World War. It has emerged fitter and leaner from the 1991-4 Champagne crisis.

The standard Brut NV is fresh and racy, with a fine mineral-like character. The bone-dry Ultra Brut has no hint of asperity, as it is always made from the grapes of a ripe year (currently 1989). Also, an immensely successful *rosé* – big and vinous; and the sumptuous Cuvée Grand Siècle, usually a blend of three years.

Albert le Brun
51000 Châlons-en-Champagne ☆☆

One of the few Châlons-based Champagne houses, Albert le Brun has been making a range of very respectable wines in full bodied, spicy styles for many years.

Look out for the ripe and smoky Blanc de Blancs from the firm's own vineyards at Avize; and the big Pinot-dominated *rosé*, Vieille France – ideal with smoked salmon.

Le Brun de Neuville
CM 51260 Bethon ☆☆

The brand name of the Bethon cooperative situated in the lesser-recognised region of the Côte Sézanne.

Seriously good Chardonnay Champagnes, and at keen prices. The British supermarket chain Sainsburys often buys wine from here.

Leclerc-Briant
NM 51204 Epernay ☆☆☆

This family firm has 30 hectares of fine vineyards, and is run with flair and passion by Pascal Leclerc-Briant.

Collection Les Authentiques is a series of Champagnes made from small parcels of vines in specific sites, in a vinous, near-Burgundian style. Generally very low *dosage*.

Marie-Noelle Ledru
RM 51150 Ambonnay ☆☆

From a *domaine* of six hectares on the Grand Cru hillsides of Ambonnay and Bouzy, Madame Ledru makes a powerful Brut – suffused with the red-fruits flavours of great Pinot Noir, and judiciously balanced with just the right amount of Chardonnay. The same wine can also be found in an Extra Brut version.

R & L Legras
NM 51530 Chouilly ☆☆☆

Having been *vignerons* since the 18th century, the Legras family became merchants in 1972.

The fine floral Grand Cru Blanc de Blancs is the house Champagne of many Michelin-starred restaurants in France. The Brut Intègral was one of the first sugarless Champagnes released in the 1970s. The vintage-dated Cuvée St Vincent is fresh, yet richly evolved.

Lemaire-Fourny
RM 51480 Damery ☆☆

This *récoltant-manipulant* makes a Blanc de Noirs from mainly Pinot Meunier grapes (85 per cent) grown in a little vineyard above Damery.

This is a good example of how good a Pinot Meunier-driven wine can be when carefully vinified.

A R Lenoble
NM 51480 Damery ☆☆☆to☆☆☆☆

This family business of growers and merchants is one of the best kept secrets in Champagne. The firm rarely advertises itself but the wines, which are sourced from an 18-hectare estate, are top flight. After tasting the Grand Cru Blanc de Blancs 1990 blind for *Decanter* magazine in July

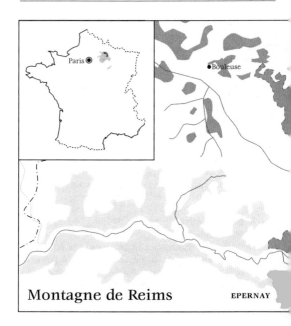

Montagne de Reims

EPERNAY

1997, my notes read, "a fresh undeveloped and slightly reductive nose; richer on the palate with a creamy *mousse* and good balance ☆☆☆☆".

Joseph Loriot
RM 51700 Festigny ☆☆☆

Festigny, in the heart of Pinot Meunier country, is home to this remarkable grower and Champagne maker. His Carte d'Or is a generous and golden, black-grapes Champagne – ample but refined, balanced and sparingly dosed. Also a finely poised Blanc de Blancs.

Michel Maillart
RM 51500 Ecueil ☆☆☆

An admired Remois grower and winemaker, Monsieur Maillart creates some of the most expressive Pinot Noir Champagnes available.

They are generously flavoured, beautifully balanced and intriguingly complex. Also an excellent vintage-dated *rosé* and Brut Prestige.

Mailly Grand Cru
CM 51500 Mailly-Champagne ☆☆*to*☆☆☆

This well-known cooperative was founded in 1929 and has 70 members, farming 70 hectares of vines exclusively within

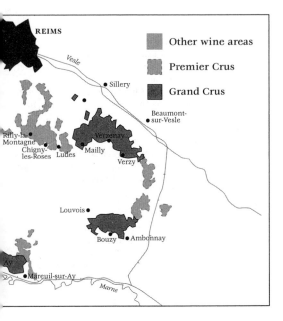

the Grand Cru of Mailly. On the whole, one either likes or dislikes the young and punchy Pinot Noir-dominated style of these Champagnes.

The Grand Cru Brut Réserve is full of primary fruit; and the Coteaux Champenois Rouge is usually excellent.

Sadi Malot
RM 51380 Villers-Marmery ☆☆☆

A leading grower and Champagne maker of Villers-Marmery with ten hectares of vines. Sadi Malot is perhaps the best exponent of Chardonnay-led *cuvées* in the village.

These are Champagnes to savour, with real complexity beyond their initial pure-flavoured fruit. The vintage-dated Cuvée SM Blanc de Blancs is usually a ☆☆☆☆ wine – the 1995 is likely to be a great bottle to enjoy in the early years of the 21st century.

Henri Mandois
RM 51530 Pierry ☆☆☆

A sizeable 30-hectare estate, where the younger generation has husbanded some very good Chardonnay and Pinot Meunier vines to produce an attractive style of Champagne.

The best seen is the Cuvée Réserve – at once supple, yet fine, racy and poised. This is Champagne making with an admirably light touch.

Armand Margaine
RM 51380 Villers-Marmery ☆☆

Armand Margaine's great grandfather started this vineyard in the early 1900s. Today it extends to seven hectares, and is planted with significant amounts of Chardonnay – the variety which excels in this commune.

His vintage-dated Special Club is dominated by the great white grape (excellent 1995 and 1989).

Marguet-Bonnerave
RM 51500 Ambonnay ☆☆

Well-established growers with 13 hectares of vines. Evolved, ripe but well-balanced style of Champagnes across the board, from a Blanc de Blanc to the Cuvée Privilege.

Marie Stuart
NM 51100 Reims ☆☆

Right in the centre of the city near the Porte du Mars, this house until recently had a workman-like reputation for making Buyers Own Brand (BOB) Champagnes.

Under the new ownership of Alain Thienot (qv), the quality has greatly improved. The opulent Cuvée de la Reine is recommended.

Serge Mathieu
RM 10349 Avirey-Lingey ☆☆☆

At this immaculate *domaine* based in the Aube, Serge Mathieu makes sensuous Champagnes of real class.

The Cuvée Select is richly mature but vitally fresh; the Brut *rosé* is sumptuous yet superfine. Older vintages of his Coteaux Champenois Rouge are little gems.

Mercier
NM 51333 Epernay ☆☆

Part of the LVMH group, this large house has extensive vineyard holdings of 218 hectares in the Marne Valley.

Always good value for money, these are well-made easy-drinking Champagnes in a soft black fruits style, shaped by a significant percentage of Pinot Meunier in the blend. Both the *rosé* and the Demi-Sec have a nice touch of unctiousness without being cloying. The Cuvée du Fondateur, driven by the two Pinots, is the best wine of all.

De Méric
NM 51160 Aÿ ☆☆

A small grower and merchant house, founded in 1960 by Christian Besserat, with a vineyard of 15 hectares at Aÿ.

The Sélection Brut is dry, structured and Pinot Noir led. Also, stylish poised Blanc de Blancs and uncompromisingly mouthfilling and vinous prestige Catherine de Medici.

Guy Michel
RM 51350 Moussy ☆☆

A Moussy grower with 20 hectares in the Cubry valley. Fine exponent of unusual Pinot Meunier and Chardonnay blends – supple, spicy and racy. Interesting older vintages.

Moët & Chandon
NM 51333 Epernay ☆☆☆

By far the biggest Champagne house producing 21-million bottles a year, Moët maintains a very high standard across the range. The various *cuvées* have a consistent style that is elegant, light and easy to drink, but also rounds out nicely with age. Very wide sources of supply make for consistency in the huge quantities of Brut Imperial NV produced.

The Premier Cru, launched in 1996, is made from better-class grapes and carries an innovative back label explaining how the wine is made. The supple and creamy house style shows best in the vintage Champagnes (1986, 1988 and 1990 all excellent).

The prestige Dom Pérignon is a truly sumptuous wine – a marvel of floral aromas, supple middle palate and great complexity. Such is the demand that the current vintage of Dom Pérignon is 1993, as yet an unsung year but likely to give a great deal of pleasure in the early 21st century.

Pierre Moncuit
RM 51190 Le Mesnil-sur-Oger ☆☆☆

Yves and Nicole Moncuit own 20 hectares in the best part of Le Mesnil, arguably the greatest *cru* of the Côte des Blancs.

Their talent is as big as their birthright, with a range of incisive, beautifully made Blanc de Blancs. The vintage trio, 1988, 1989 and 1990, are excellent representatives of their respective years.

Montaudon
NM 51100 Reims ☆☆

Established in 1891, the firm is managed by Luc Montaudon, the great grandson of the founder. Essentially a Pinot Noir house with 20 hectares, mainly on the Montagne de Reims.

Good long-lived Grande Réserve rosé; structured vintage wines (1989); and interesting Coteaux Champenois Rouge.

Jean Moutardier
NM 51210 Le Breuil ☆☆☆

Moutardier's English son-in-law, Jonathon Saxby, makes excellent Pinot Meunier-based Champagnes at this 16-hectare estate, south of Dormans.

The rich and powerful 1990 (100 per cent Pinot Meunier) dispels the myth that great Champagne is exclusively made from Pinot Noir and Chardonnay.

Yves Mouzon
RM 51380 Verzy ☆☆

If you find many Champagnes are too finely honed at the expense of character, try this Verzy-grower's Grande Réserve: with its scent of wood smoke and its spicy, mature Pinot flavours. This is a fine Champagne to partner Cantonese duck with star anise.

Mumm
NM 51000 Reims ☆☆

It is hard to generalise about the style and quality of Mumm Champagnes as the range is very wide. For several years the Cordon Rouge NV has been one of the least impressive from the *grandes maisons* – dull, young tasting and not always in balance. All that could now change.

In 1997 a new *chef de caves*, Dominique Demarvais, was appointed and his first *cuvée* (blended in spring 1998) is impressive, powerful, full of raspberry fruitiness, long flavoured and with fine acidity. The Mumm de Cramant is a delicate, pure, Chardonnay Champagne made from Grand Cru Cramant grapes from a single year.

The best of the vintage wines is the Grand Cordon prestige *cuvée*; with a steely long-flavour and a slight majority of Chardonnay (excellent 1990).

Napoléon
NM 51130 Vertus NM ☆☆☆

The brand name of traditionalist bijou house, Prieur. The Tradition Carte d'Or NV is a gem – elegant, yet rich and beautifully balanced. Excellent value for money.

Oudinot
NM 51207 Epernay ☆☆

Founded in the late 19th-century, this house has been owned by the Trouillard brothers since 1981.

Ultra-modern winemaking produces clean and well-made Champagnes – the floral Brut NV and expansively flavoured Blanc de Noirs are recommended. They own 80 hectares of vineyards, with fine sites in Avize, Chouilly and Cramant.

Bruno Paillard
NM 51100 Reims ☆☆☆

The youngest classic Champagne house, founded in 1981 by Bruno Paillard, a broker with an impressive knowledge of the industry. These are Champagnes for connoisseurs – elegant, structured and very dry.

Particular care is lavished on the outstanding Première Cuvée NV; only the first pressings of the grapes are used and the wines are part-fermented (20 per cent) in wood. The excellent vintage Champagnes, each year illustrated by a

prominent artist, carry the date of disgorging (superb 1990).
Bruno Paillard is involved in a group financing other houses
such as Boizel, Chanoine and Philipponat (qqv).

Palmer
CM 51100 Reims ☆☆☆

One of the best cooperatives in Champagne, Palmer is small
enough to concentrate on quality. Winemaking is never
hurried, and the Champagnes are rested for three to six
months after dégorgement.

Both the 1988 Blanc de Blancs and the prestige *cuvée*
Amazone are exceptional. Excellent ratio of quality to price.

Pannier
CM 02430 Château-Thierry ☆☆☆

An excellent cooperative of growers cultivating 410 hectares,
mainly in the Marne Valley, but also with access to grapes
from the Montagne de Reims and Côte des Blancs.

The standard Brut Tradition is dominated by Pinot
Meunier and gives a supple, pleasurable Champagne. The
Cuvée Louis Eugene (60 per cent Pinot Meunier and 40 per
cent Chardonnay) is finer and more structured. Excellent
1990 vintage sustained by fine acidity. Good value.

Joseph Perrier
NM 51000 Châlons-en-Champagne ☆☆☆

Now part-owned by Laurent-Perrier, this fine house was
founded in 1825 and is a very sure source of classic
Champagnes made by traditional methods, with no short
cuts. This firm own 20 hectares around Cumières, Damery,
Hautvillers and Verneuil.

The grapes – essentially the two Pinots – shape the
succulent, ripe house style of the Cuvée Royale NV, but the
flavours are never overblown thanks to brilliant blending
with Chardonnay. The 1990 vintage, released in 1998, steers
a perfect middle course between richness and freshness.

Perrier-Jouët
NM 51200 Epernay ☆☆to☆☆☆

Founded in 1811, Perrier-Jouët owed its top-flight reputation
for many years to the tasting skills of the late Michel Budin,
whose father bought the company in the 1930s.

Although nowadays one has to pick and choose the best
cuvées, the firm's strong card remains its superb 75 hectares
of vineyards, which include great Chardonnay sites on the
Côte des Blancs. These vineyards shape the creamy-hazelnut
style of the straight vintage Champagnes (excellent 1990)
which offer the best buys here. Fine Blason de France *rosé*.

The prestige Belle Epoque 1985 was a very great wine
and priced accordingly.

Philipponnat

NM 51160 Mareuil-sur-Aÿ ☆☆☆

A small traditional firm, sold in 1998 by Marie Brizard to a group headed by Bruno Paillard.

To date, good to excellent mellow Pinot-led Champagnes culminating in the superb single-vineyard Clos des Goisses – invariably a powerful concentrated *cuvée* (brilliant 1988 and 1985), this wine has a vinosity to match game or mature gruyère cheese.

Pierre Peters

RM 51190 Le Mesnil-sur-Oger ☆☆☆

Francis Peters is now at the helm of this 17-hectare estate with prime plots in and around Le Mesnil.

His top *cuvée*, the Mesnil Blanc de Blancs, is a first-rate example of this great vineyard, with white-flowers aromas and a complex evolved Burgundian vinosity on the palate. First tastings of the Chardonnay wines of the 1995 vintage suggest this will be a fine year for the house.

Ployez-Jacquemart

NM 51500 Ludes ☆☆

This boutique Champagne house owns a couple of well-sited hectares, but buys in most of its grapes to produce a good, classic-style Chardonnay and Pinot Noir Brut; a stylish Blanc de Blancs; and, in exceptional years, the wood-fermented Cuvée Liesse d'Harbonville. There are no reserve wines used in the blends.

Pol Gessner

NM 51200 Epernay ☆☆

One of many labels of the giant Marne et Champagne group, Pol Gessner is often reserved for better *cuvées* with more age in bottle. The Réserve is a reliable Champagne.

Pol Roger

NM 51200 Epernay ☆☆☆☆

This is probably the most consistently exciting *grande marque*; in fact, Pol Roger is seemingly incapable of making a bottle of Champagne that is not utterly delicious.

The White Foil NV is the perfect Champagne – light yet structured, fresh and floral, but surprisingly complex. How is it done? The family still decide on the blend, but have the good sense to employ James Coffinet, a brilliant *chef de caves* and pioneer of the "cold settling" technique (qv).

The vintage Champagnes of this house are incomparably subtle and long-lived in style. Best of all is also the least-known Cuvée Spéciale PR – a classic blend of Grand Cru Pinot Noir and Chardonnay fruit. The 1988 is a marvel of richness and exquisite balance.

Pommery
NM 51100 Reims ☆☆☆

This house was founded in 1836 by another famous widow Louise Pommery. It has always been a potentially fine *grande marque* with a magnificent vineyard area of 295 hectares in the best sites, and is at last turning that potential into reality. The LVMH group took over control of Pommery in 1990.

The Brut Royale NV has now become a fine, notably dry Champagne of low *dosage*. The 1991 vintage, released in 1998, is both subtle and concentrated; the prestige *cuvée* Louise (classic 1988) is first rate, with a lingering vinosity. There are also magnums of late disgorged older vintages under the Flacons d'Exception label (outstanding 1979).

Virgile Portier
RM 51360 Beaumont-sur-Vesle ☆☆

This Montagne de Reims grower makes a very good Brut Spéciale – a classic *assemblage* of Pinot Noir and Chardonnay (no Pinot Meunier). It is a mouthfilling wine – rich but harmonious, with the aromas and flavours of orchard fruits, and a nice touch of maturity.

Pascal Redon
RM 51380 Trépail ☆☆*to*☆☆☆

A gifted winemaker, Pascal Redon has produced his own Champagne from six hectares of Premier Cru grapes since the early 1980s.

Typical of a Trépail *domaine*, Chardonnay dominates the blends in the Brut, the exceptional *rosé*, and the vintage *cuvée* (fine 1995 for future reference).

Renaudin
RM 51530 Moussy ☆☆

An important grower and winemaker with 24 hectares at Moussy, Renaudin makes stylish Champagnes dominated by Chardonnay, but also with the softening touch of quick-maturing Pinots.

These Champagnes make an excellent *apéritif* style or late afternoon reviver.

Alain Robert
RM 51190 Le Mesnil-sur-Oger ☆☆☆☆

From an old family of growers who came to Le Mesnil in the 17th century, Alain Robert is a driven perfectionist. He owns 12 hectares, in seven villages of the Côte des Blancs, and makes only pure Chardonnay Champagne.

None of his *cuvées* are released until they are seven years old. His top-of-the-range Le Mesnil, which spends a decade on lees, is a magnificent mouthful of evolved Chardonnay flavours – *sans pareil*.

Louis Roederer
NM 51100 Reims ☆☆☆☆

Top-draw, family owned Champagne house run with a mix of wine passion and business acumen by Jean-Claude Rouzaud, a trained oenologist and proud of it.

Roederer's peerless reputation and financial soundness rests on its superb vineyards of 180 hectares which supply 70 per cent of its needs, controlled sales (2.6 million bottles a year) and perfectionist winemaking. For example, the reserve wines for the notably smooth and rich Brut Premier NV (60 per cent Pinot Noir) are aged in wood, giving a honeyed vanillin style to this *cuvée*.

Other gems include the pale-coloured, subtly vinous *rosé*; the rare, gently sparkling Blanc de Blancs; and the fabulous Cristal – this, the most sought-after prestige *cuvée* of all, with particularly splendid vintages in 1985 and 1989.

(*See* also Roederer Estate, California).

Royer Père et fils
RM 10110 Landreville ☆☆

A relatively new Aube *domaine,* first established in the 1960s, now with 17 hectares of vines. Good aromatic and full-bodied Champagnes – be it the Pinot Noir-dominated Brut or the pure-Chardonnay Blanc de Blancs.

Alfred Rothschild
NM 51200 Epernay ☆☆

The upmarket brand of the Marne et Champagne group, usually reserved for *cuvées* with a high Chardonnay content.

The Blanc de Blancs NV is usually a fine, long-flavoured wine, skillfully blended with *crus* from the Côtes des Blancs and Sézanne. Good quality-to-price ratio.

Ruelle-Pertois
RM 51530 Moussy ☆☆

Michel Ruelle-Pertois' grandfather planted this vineyard, which now extends to six hectares in size. Essentially he is a Chardonnay producer, with a very good Réserve Blanc de Blancs – usually a blend of two mature years and at least six years on the lees. Good rapport of quality and price.

Ruinart
NM 51000 Reims ☆☆☆☆

Founded in 1729, this is the oldest recorded Champagne house, and makes elegant, richly textured wines.

The prestige Dom Ruinart is a most distinguished Blanc de Blancs – silky, full and rounded due to the Montagne de Reims Chardonnays in the blend (fine 1988). The Dom Ruinart *rosé* (especially the 1986) is equally outstanding. The new "R" *rosé*, replacing the older, simpler style of *rosé*, dispenses with Pinot Meunier in the blend, while favouring a majority of Chardonnay over Pinot Noir.

Salon
NM 51190 Le Mesnil-sur-Oger ☆☆☆☆

Salon is the only house to produce just one type of Champagne – always a Blanc de Blancs, always vintage dated and only released a couple of times a decade, when the wine is thought worthy of its awesome reputation. The aromas recall walnuts, the flavours are richly fruity but with strong acidity to ensure a very long life.

Of recent vintages, the 1983 will be followed by the 1988 and 1990 before the 1985, which tells you a lot about the house's rating of each vintage in the pecking order!

Camille Saves
RM 51150 Bouzy ☆☆

This nine-hectare *domaine* has a modern, pristine cellar. One associates Bouzy with Pinot Noir, but Chardonnay (65 per cent) is dominant here in the Cuvée de Réserve – a fine, big Champagne with mouth-coating flavours of dried fruits such as apricots. The Pinot Noir (35 per cent) adds a useful punch to the end flavour.

Jacques Selosse
RM 51190 Avize ☆☆☆☆

Avize grower Anselme Selosse learned the art of winemaking in Beaune, and his originality has been to apply the hand-made approach of classic white burgundy making to the more technical world of Champagne.

Here the wines are fermented in wood and the lees stirred once a week with a baton, as in Meursault. They offer a compact range of superbly complex Champagnes, which are full of *gras* and savour.

Brilliant bone-dry Extra Brut, and fabulous smokey, spicy Cuvée d'Origine fermented in new oak barriques.

Cristian Senez
NM 10360 Fontette ☆☆

An important grower in the Aube and resourceful winemaker, producing a range of good Champagnes in a fine "dancing" style. A remarkable collection of older vintages, back to 1973.

Also youthful, easy-drinking Coteaux Champenois Rouge, by carbonic maceration.

Serge Billiot
RM 51150 Ambonnay ☆☆☆to☆☆☆☆

A grower who makes only minute quantities of remarkable Champagne, culminating in the superb Cuvée Laetitia – a multi-vintage blend.

Alain Soutiran-Pelletier

RM 51150 Ambonnay ☆☆

Alain Soutiran nows runs this little *domaine,* which has been making its own Champagnes since the mid-1970s.

Two recommended *cuvées* in contrasting styles: a full and expansive Blanc de Noir made from 100-per-cent-rated Pinot Noir grapes, and a rounded and balanced vintage-dated Blanc de Blancs. Good quality.

Taillevent

MA 75008 Paris ☆☆☆

A BOB with a difference, for this is the fabled Taillevent restaurant's very own Champagne. A vintage-dated wine, it is always made by Maison Deutz (qv), a ☆☆☆☆ *grande marque* based in Aÿ. There is a white and a *rosé,* both structured Champagnes for great *cuisine.*

Taittinger

NM 51061 Reims ☆☆*to*☆☆☆

Although this famous house can trace its origins back to the 18th century, it is only since 1945 that it has become one of the most important forces in Champagne.

Throughout its expansion Taittinger has bought excellent vineyards, and its current holdings of 260 hectares are predominantly Chardonnay sites in the Côte des Blancs and the Aube. The floral, toasty house style is best shown in the Brut Réserve. Greatly improved in the late 1990s, it still retains a noticeable *dosage.*

The prestige Comtes de Champagne is a marvellous Chardonnay Champagne – tasting steely and austere when young, it develops a splendid "burgundian" richness with age (great in 1982, 1985 and 1988). Taittinger also owns the sparkling wine concerns of Bouvey Ladubay in the Loire and Domaine Carneros in California (qqv).

Tanneux-Mahy

RM 51530 Mardeuil ☆☆

Jacques Tanneux cultivates six hectares just west of Epernay, and is best known for his succulent and full-flavoured Cuvée Les Chasseurs. This is a Champagne, dominated by black grapes, for the ravenous hunter to drink with cold pheasant when he breaks for lunch after a morning on the hill.

Tarlant

RM 51480 Oeuilly ☆☆☆*to*☆☆☆☆

A top-flight grower with 13 hectares in the Marne Valley, he vinifies the wines from individual vineyards separately to give best expression to their respective soils. The Brut Zéro is one of the best bone-dry Champagnes on the market, and the Krug-like Cuvée Louis, fermented in new oak, is outstanding.

de Telmont
NM 51480 Damery ☆☆

Dynamic growers and merchants with a 30-hectare vineyard in the Marne Valley. Sales in excess of one million bottles a year. Good quality at very fair prices generally, especially the Brut and the vintage-dated Blanc de Blancs (fine 1993).

Alain Thiénot
NM 51100 Reims ☆☆☆

Broker turned merchant, Alain Thiénot is a dynamic force for good in Champagne. The firm owns 14 hectares, mainly at Aÿ and Le Mesnil-sur-Oger. The wines are rather like Alain himself – natural, vital and with great strength of character.

His skilled blending of all three Champagne grapes results in a fresh, supple, but structured Brut NV; a fine, very dry vintage *rosé*; and an outstanding Grande Cuvée 1990 – of beautiful gold colour, toasty aromas and rich long flavours, balanced by excellent acidity.

Union Champagne
CM 51190 Avize ☆☆☆☆

The leader in quality of all the Champagne cooperatives, its member growers own magnificent Chardonnay plots on the Côte des Blancs. The winemaking is immaculate, and malolactic fermentation is avoided to ensure a long life.

The Cuvée Orpale 1985 was the bargain of the decade among the top Blanc de Blancs.

Veuve A Devaux
CM 10110 Bar-sur-Seine ☆☆to☆☆☆

The leading brand label of the powerful Union Auboise cooperative, now well established in the UK and USA. It shows very assured winemaking, but the Aube character of the finished Champagnes can be muted.

Their best *cuvées* include the first-rate Grande Réserve – evolved, spicy and delicious; plus the lovely '88 Rosé.

Veuve Fourny
NM 51130 Vertus ☆☆to☆☆☆

A promising Blanc de Blancs producer with seven hectares, including some 60-year-old vines in the single-vineyard "Clos Notre Dame". A vigorous, incisive style of real finesse.

Marcel Vezien
RM 10110 Celles-sur-Ource ☆☆☆

These are full, lush Champagnes and typify the best of the Aube. The Cuvée Double Eagle 11 is a hedonistic Pinot mouthful, and was named after American balloonists who celebrated their safe arrival on French soil with a bottle of this very nectar.

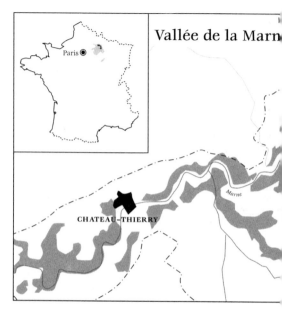

Vilmart

RM 51500 Rilly-la-Montagne ☆☆to☆☆☆☆

This tiny firm makes the Grand Cellier d'Or, wood-fermented and wonderful, with a whiff of ginger bread and a honeyed opulence – truly a ☆☆☆☆ Champagne.

The new Coeur de Cuvée, fermented in new-oak barriques can taste overly wooded, and there have been complaints about the consistency of the standard Grande Réserve. Taste before buying.

Vollereaux

NM 51530 Pierry ☆☆

Growers and merchants in the Cubry Valley since the end of the Great War (1919), Vollereaux have a sizeable 40-hectare vineyard, but also buy grapes in. Good quality Chardonnay-led wines, especially from the underrated 1993 vintage.

Vranken

NM 51200 Epernay (see individual houses also)

Corporate raider of the 1990s, Paul-Francois Vranken is not loved by the *grandees* of Champagne. His rapidly expanding group includes Barancourt, Demoiselle, and Charles Lafitte (qqv), each decent Champagne houses in their category. Vranken has also revitalised the ailing *grande marque*, Heidsieck Monopole. Watch this space....

Legend:
- -·- Area Outline
- Other wine areas
- Premier Crus

Villers-sous-Chatillon
Hautvillers
Damery · Cumières
·Leuvrigny · Dizy
Mardeuil ·
EPERNAY
Tours-sur-Marne ·
Marne
voisy

Other French sparkling wine

Outside Champagne, a welcome trend is the increasing variety of well-made sparkling *crémant* wines available from the classic regions of France. The best *crémants* come from Alsace and, when carefully selected, from the Loire.

Areas including Burgundy, Bordeaux, Limoux, Die (near the Rhone) and, most recently, Jura, now also have their own regional *crémant* appellations. Each has strict rules stipulating lower yields; better grapes; a gentler once-only pressing of the harvest; and, crucially, longer ageing on lees. Quality is on the up and this whole area is a happy hunting ground for palatable fizz at friendly prices.

ALSACE

Sparkling wine has been made in Alsace since the turn of the century, albeit on a tiny scale for many years. The creation of the appellation Crémant d'Alsace in 1976 was the necessary impetus for the production of Champagne-method sparklers in serious commercial quantities.

In the period 1976–1996, the total volume of Crémant d'Alsace had increased from 1 million to 14.6 million litres a year, much of it drunk in the smart cafés of Strasbourg and Paris. Quality is good and getting better as a new breed of talented smaller growers apply a handmade approach to a product that was previously the domain of large cooperatives and merchant houses. The main grape varieties used to make this *crémant* are Pinot Blanc and Auxerrois. Pinot Gris and Riesling can also add structure and complexity; and much hope has been placed in the fashionable Chardonnay. However, it may be Pinot Noir that is to prove the most promising grape of all, with the potential to make a range of Blanc de Noirs in Alsace that truly sing.

Allimant-Laugner
67600 Orschiller ☆☆

A ten-hectare *domaine* run by the talented and enthusiastic Hubert Laugner. His 1994 is subtle and well balanced – a nice touch of maturity in harmony with its orchard fruit flavours.

Anstolz
67310 Balbronn ☆☆

In the north of the Bas-Rhin, on ideal chalky soils, the Anstolz family makes a good *crémant* with elegant little bubbles. A steely definition of flavour is given by the Riesling in the blend, and a respectably long finish.

Cave Vinicole de Beblenheim
68630 Beblenheim ☆

One of Alsace's largest cooperatives with over 200 members farming 220 hectares. A high-volume production of young *crémant*, in the main, based on Auxerrois and Pinot Blanc.

The wines are of fair quality, but in a different league is the Baron de Hoen, Blanc de Noirs 1994 – a fine expression of supple and succulent Pinot Noir.

Bernard Becht
671120 Dorlisheim ☆☆

In the pretty Bas-Rhin village of Dorlisheim (the Romanesque church is worth a visit) Monsieur Becht makes 5,000 bottles a year of fine sparkling wine. They show regular small bubbles, expressive Pinot aromas, good weight and poised presence in the mouth and a serious persistent finish.

Cave Coopérative de Bennwihr
68630 Bennwihr ☆

A big Alsace coop taking growers' grapes from Bennwihr and surrounding villages in this part of the Haut-Rhin. Sound and basic Crémant d'Alsace at reasonable prices.

Emile Beyer
68420 Eguisheim ☆☆

Close to the Château d'Eguisheim in a beautiful 16th-century building, this firm makes a fine *crémant* with aromas of white flowers and flavours of white peaches. Finesse, elegance and harmony are the keynotes.

Other French sparkling wine areas

Wine areas

1. (Champagne)
2. Crémant d'Alsace
3. Crémant de Bourgogne
4. Crémant de Loire
5. Crémant de Jura
6. Crémant de Bordeaux
7. St-Péray
8. Clairette and Crémant de Die
9. Blanquette and Crémant de Limoux

Maison Blanck
68420 Kayserberg ☆☆☆

Kayserberg is a handsome little town surrounded by some of the best vineyards in Alsace. Of the many Blancks in the commune, this branch, headed by brothers Bernard and Marcel and their sons Frederic and Philippe, makes the best wines, including stunning still Riesling.

They produce Crémant d'Alsace in two versions: Brut and Brut Sauvage (without *dosage*). Both wines are made from two-thirds Pinot Blanc and one-third Pinot Gris and Riesling – the Riesling giving real class to the *cuvée*. A new Chardonnay vineyard is just coming on stream.

Emile Boeckel
67140 Mittelbergheim ☆☆

This is a sizeable merchant house, founded at the turn of the century. But, it has only been producing sparkling wine since 1980.

The grapes for the *crémant* come from the firm's own vineyard in Mittelbergheim where, in addition to Pinot Blanc and Auxerrois, some Chardonnay is planted. Very good Brut Extra (full Chardonnay) – elegant and long flavoured.

Cave Vinicole de Cleeborg
671046 Cleebourg ☆☆

In the far north of the Bas-Rhin, just a few minutes drive from Strasbourg, the vineyards belonging to this cooperative are mainly planted with Pinot Gris.

The best *cuvée* of *crémant* here is The Clerotstein 1994 – showing the ample richness of the Pinot Gris. A good sparkler for the first course of a meal.

Dopff "Au Moulin"
68340 Riquewihr ☆☆

One of the most distinguished *grandes maisons* in Alsace, its history dates back to the late 16th-century. They are the main exporters – selling nearly one million bottles of *crémant* a year worldwide. Their own vineyards are mainly Pinot Blanc, and supply around a third of their grape requirements. The rest is bought in under contract from local growers.

The Blanc de Noirs and vintage-dated Cuvée Bartholdi (half and half Pinot Blanc and Pinot Noir) are particularly recommended from the large range.

Dopff & Irion
68340 Riquewihr ☆

Probably Alsace's largest merchant shipper, Dopff & Irion makes a relatively modest quantity of *crémant*, some 170,000 bottles a year. It buys in mainly Pinot Blanc and Auxerrois for its sparklers, which are acceptable, if unexciting.

Cave Vinicole d'Eguisheim
68420 Eguisheim ☆☆

Under the able direction of Pierre Hussherr, this vast cooperative is the most important producer of Crémant d'Alsace (up to 4.8 million bottles a year under the Wolfberger label). Decent quality – occasionally excellent: the Extra Brut 1994 (half and half Pinot Blanc and Pinot Noir) is fresh, yet nicely mature, with good length.

Fernand Engel et fils
68590 Rorschwihr ☆☆

With an estate of more than 30 hectares, the Engels are one of the most important families of growers in the Haut-Rhin.

From predominantly Chardonnay vines, they produce a very good *crémant* – floral and racy, with a harmonious fruit-to-acid balance.

Victor Hertz
68420 Herrlisheim ☆☆☆

Having vineyards that are placed in three choice communes (especially Wintzenheim), this house makes 4,000 bottles of excellent vintage-dated Crémant d'Alsace a year.

The 1994 is exceptional, with a ripe, golden colour and marked depth and concentration of flavours.

Kieffer
67140 Itterswiller ☆☆☆

Jean-Charles and Damien Kieffer come from an old family of growers who settled in Itterswiller in the 18th century.

Their Blanc de Noirs 1994 has an expressive scent of red fruits and a deliciously fruity, yet surprisingly complex flavour, typical of Pinot Noir. An adaptable *crémant,* either as an *apéritif* or with food.

Marc Kreydenweiss
67140 Andlau ☆☆

Based in the picturesque village of Andlau, opposite the fine old church, Marc Kreydenweiss is one of the new breed of growers; making exceptional still Riesling, Pinot Gris and Auxerrois which are listed at Le Crocodile – recognised as Strasbourg's best restaurant.

His Crémant d'Alsace is pretty good too, and sourced from the same grapes.

Muré
68250 Rouffach ☆☆

In a pretty village off the *route des vins* in the southern Haut-Rhin, this is a traditional family business whose pride and joy is the Clos St Landelin vineyard. The wines for its range of *crémants* are classically fermented and aged in large oak *foudres*. The Cuvée Prestige Muré Brut is a good wine, deriving its richness from a significant proportion of Pinot Gris, as well as Pinot Blanc and Auxerrois, in the blend.

Pierre Sparr
68240 Sigolsheim ☆☆☆

A respected family of growers and merchants, the seventh and eighth generations now working in this solid business.

High standards of vinification and blending are employed in composing their *crémants* – at least two or three vintages are usually used in the basic *cuvées* to obtain a consistent style. The 1994 Blanc de Noirs, a real Champagne alternative, has a *cordon* of tiny elegant bubbles; fine definition of red fruits flavours; and is at once fresh and honeyed.

Cave Coopérative de Turckheim
68230 Turckheim ☆☆☆

Like everything else from this outstanding cooperative, the Crémant d'Alsace made under the Mayerling label, is excellent. Made from a classic half and half blend of Pinot Blanc and Auxerrois, this is a splendidly sprightly wine and very refreshing on a hot summer's evening. About 25,000 cases are produced, and it is very good value.

Pierre-Paul Zink
68250 Pfaffenheim ☆☆

This dedicated family of growers started to make Crémant d'Alsace in 1983. Usually wines of a single year, the *crémants* are very fresh and clean tasting, and of model balance.

THE LOIRE

Along its course of more than 600 miles, from the centre of France to the Atlantic ocean, the river Loire is home to a variety of sparkling wines, both white and *rosé*. The main areas of production are Anjou, Saumur and Touraine – the central Loire Valley – whence about 24-million bottles of good Champagne-method sparklers find their way each year onto French and foreign markets.

Light, refreshing and inexpensive, they make good party fizz, but rarely rise to match the quality of Champagne in the way that the better *crémant* producers of Alsace increasingly do. The main problem for the Loire is a multiplicity of grape varieties ill-suited to the making of fine sparkling wine.

The Crémant de Loire appellation, introduced in 1975, was supposed to usher in a better class of Loire sparkling wine. Several of its provisions, such as an insistence on hand-harvesting of the grapes and longer ageing on lees, made good sense. But, the pot pourri of permitted grape varieties and the restriction on Chardonnay plantings mitigate against finesse. The best Loire sparklers are made from pure Chenin

Blanc by the serious big houses and cooperatives of Saumur, and by small growers in Vouvray and Montlouis, where Chenin Blanc is the sole permitted variety.

Aime Boucher
37210 Vouvray ☆☆

A large sparkling wine merchant drawing grapes from many parts of the central Loire. In general the wines are of good quality – including sparkling Vouvray and Crémant de Loire, which are recommended.

Ackerman Laurance
49400 St-Hilaire-St-Florent ☆☆☆

The most important sparkling-wine producer in Saumur, still using the deep limestone caves excavated in 1811 by the founder, Jean Ackerman.

High quality for such a vast operation. Fresh and floral 1811 Saumur; a lovely *rosé*; and the very impressive luxury Privilege – lightly wooded, with a burgeoning vinosity. A serious Champagne alternative.

Domaines des Baumard
49190 Rochefort-sur-Loire ☆☆

The Baumards are best known for their excellent still Savennières Clos du Papillon. The Carte Corail is a fine pink *crémant* of beautiful rose-petal colour, elegant *mousse* and pure fresh flavours.

Blanc Foussy
37210 Rochecorbon ☆

A leading high-volume brand of Touraine sparkling wine, the Vin Vif de Touraine accounts for 1.75 million bottles a year in Brut, Demi-Sec and *rosé* versions. Fair quality, not expensive.

Their top wine, Cuvée des Comtes de Touraine, helped by Chardonnay, is good.

Bouvet Ladubay
49400 St-Hilaire-St-Florent ☆☆☆

Owned by Champagne Taittinger since 1974, Bouvet is the second-oldest house in Saumur. The better-quality *cuvées* are first rate. The Excellence, a fine example of sparkling Chenin Blanc, has everything – green-gold colour; a bouquet of real finesse; and a deep flavoured yet finely balanced palate.

The luxury Trésor is serious stuff, wood-fermented and of multi-layered complexity.

Marc Bredif
37210 Rochecorbon ☆☆

The wonderful limestone caves of this reliable sparkling producer are worth a visit. A specialist in the rare and hard-to-make Vouvray *pétillant* (slightly sparkling); don't miss the chance to try it – subtle and delicious, and always with at least five years on lees.

Clos Naudin
37210 Vouvray ☆☆

Philippe Foreau is the winemaker at this 12-hectare *domaine*, which is famed for its superb dessert Vouvrays (especially the Quintessence).

The Brut sparkling Vouvray is not quite in the same league, but is a full-bodied, well-aged wine and well above the average standard.

Domaine de la Gabilliere
37400 Amboise ☆☆☆

Teacher knows best. This is the working *domaine* of the Lycée Viticole d'Amboise, where they regularly make a brilliant *crémant* – ripe, with notes of exotic fruits and a supple luxuriant texture, it's a wine for sweetbreads!

Gratien & Meyer
49401 Saumur ☆☆

Owned by the Seydoux family, whose assets include Alfred Gratien Champagne (qv). This is an important Saumur house, producing about 1.8 million bottles a year, 50 per cent of which are exported.

Gratien & Meyer does buy in most of its grapes under contract, and produces attractive Chenin-Blanc-driven Cuvée Royale, with aromas of white flowers and supple, round, long mouthfeel. An annual summer wine school also exists.

Le Clos Baudoin
37210 Vouvray ☆☆☆

This is an estate of 23 hectares, owned by Prince Poniatowki, with a peerless reputation for its fine, sweet Vouvrays.

Beautiful Aigle d'Or dry, sparkling Vouvray is highly recommended – floral; immaculately balanced; a class act. The prince also makes a Touraine *rosé* from two hectares of Cabernet Franc.

Huet, Domaine du Haut-Lieu
37210 Vouvray ☆☆☆

A family estate of the greatest reputation, run by Noël Pinguet, the son-in-law of the fabled Gaston Huet. Some of the house's procedures include the practice of biodynamic viticulture, and long slow fermentations to produce wines of great distinction.

The Vouvray *pétillant* is a fine, honeyed, but definitely dry wine; however, it is only made in quantity when the weather conditions permit.

Langlois Château
49426 St-Hiliare-St-Florent ☆☆
This house is now owned by Champagne Bollinger (qv). Both the Brut NV and the vintage Réserve are made predominantly from Chenin Blanc, with a little Chardonnay added.

Their sparkling wines are fresh, clean and flowery – ideal as *apéritifs*; but unfortunately lacking the complexity to be in the top league.

Louis de Grenelle
49415 Saumur ☆☆
Founded in 1859, this is a serious house, specialising in Champagne-method sparkling wines.

There are two recommendations – the silky, full and rounded Crémant de Loire Brut; and the excellent Saumur *rosé* – at once racy and rich, with the beautifully expressive red-fruits flavours of Cabernet Franc.

Mallard Etchegaray, Domaines des Matines
49700 Brossay ☆☆☆
A rising star of Anjou's *domaines*, making excellent Brut and *rosé* sparkling wines made by traditional methods. All are marked by elegant *cordon* bubbles, ripe clear fruit and considerable length of flavour. An estate to watch.

Caves de Vignerons de Saumur
49260 St-Cyr-en-Bourg ☆☆☆
A top cooperative of the central Loire, making excellent and immaculately vinified wines, both still and sparkling.

First rate Crémant de Loire in white and *rosé* Brut; plus the speciality of the house, the Cuvée de la Chevalerie, currently the 1993 – a high-wire act of finesse and deep peach-like flavours.

Veuve Amiot
49326 St-Hilaire-St-Florent ☆☆
Founded in 1884, a big but quality-conscious sparkling Saumur house making, about five million bottles a year.

The Crémant de Loire Brut NV is particularly good right now – light and elegant, but with a true waxy flavour of good Chenin Blanc.

CREMANT DE BOURGOGNE
Burgundy has been producing sparkling wines for more than a century. Until the mid-1970s, the appellation of Bourgogne Mousseux had a low reputation: many of the wines were dark-tinted horrors and, in general, fairly heavy, coarse and anything but fine.

In 1975 the new Crémant de Bourgogne appellation was created. This specified that only the Pinot Noir, Pinot Blanc,

Chardonnay and Aligoté grapes could be used in production. But, after a shaky start, these new Burgundy sparklers have gradually improved, particularly when made with a high proportion of Chardonnay.

Currently the best producers are growers – both private *domaines* and quality-conscious cooperative groupings – in the Mâconnais, Chalonnais and Yonne areas. It might be of interest to note that the Bourgogne Mousseux appellation was abolished in 1984.

Cave Coopérative d'Azé
71260 Azé ☆
Close to the prehistoric caves of Azé, this cooperative makes youthful *crémants*, including a fruit-laden and vintage-dated Blanc de Noirs.

Caves de Bailly
89530 St-Bris-le-Vineux ☆☆☆
An admired Auxerrois cooperative (near Chablis) known for its excellent *crémants*. The local Pinot Noir, Chardonnay and Aligoté grapes – high toned, racy and with good acidity – are an ideal base for sparkling wines.

The Meurgis Blanc de Noirs (fine 1993) could be mistaken for Champagne – minerally, supple and complex.

Georges Blanc
71260 Rizerolles ☆☆
Fabled chef Georges Blanc owns five hectares of Chardonnay at Rizerolles, from which he makes a fine Blanc de Blancs – floral, structured and long.

This is the house fizz at Vonnas – Georges Blanc's Michelin three-star restaurant across the Saône.

Bernard & Odile Cros
71390 Cercot ☆☆☆
This is a small Saône-et-Loire grower who makes 11,000 bottles a year of admirable *crémant*, and which is usually the product of a single vintage.

The 1994 is a typical *vin de vigneron* – green gold, mouthfilling, round and generous.

André Delorme
71150 Rully ☆☆
This house is a well-regarded and medium-sized shipper. André Delorme produces about half a million bottles of sparkling wine a year.

Very good vintage-dated *rosé* Brut, made predominantly from Pinot Noir – sprightly, poised, yet generously flavoured. This is an established brand in the UK, Holland, Germany and the USA.

Les Vignerons de Haute-Bourgogne
21400 Châtillon-sur-Seine ☆☆

Situated in the far north of the Côte d'Or *département*, and touching the border with the Aube, this cooperative is a find.

The Brut NV is a bargain, with finesse, body and balance. A very respectable bottle.

Cave de Lugny
71260 Lugny ☆☆☆

A leading sparkling wine producer among the Mâconnais-region's cooperatives. Self sufficient in Pinot Noir and Chardonnay grapes from its members' vineyards, it makes an admirably consistent Crémant de Bourgogne – fresh and full; and an excellent Blanc de Noirs – floral yet yeasty.

Roger Luquet
71960 Fuissé ☆☆

Better known for first-rate St-Véran and Pouilly-Fuissé, Roger Luquet also makes an individual *crémant*.

A fine expression of sparkling Chardonnay – racy and aromatic, with a hazelnut character.

Domaine des Moirots
71390 Bissey-sous-Cruchard ☆☆☆

A greatly admired Saône-et-Loire grower, making superb *crémant* from a canny mix of Pinot Noir and Aligoté, which shows splendid vibrant fruit, with a seductive round and silky mouthfeel. A marvellous accompaniment to *andouilettes* (pork chitterling sausages).

Groupement des Producteurs de Prissé
71960 Prissé ☆☆☆

A southern Mâconnais cooperative with one of the best white winemakers in Burgundy, which shows in this immaculate *crémant* – a regular flow of tiny bubbles and a citrus scent of pure Chardonnay; sprightly but gentle flavour; and a truly splendid *apéritif*.

Simmonet-Febvre
89800 Chablis ☆

A rarity, a well-known Chablis *négociant* firm, which still makes about 120,000 bottles of sparkling wine a year.

Decent quality Crémant de Bourgogne – more *pétillant* than fully sparkling – with a distinctive mineral-like and Chablis character.

Lucien Thomas, Domaine de la Feuillarde
71960 Prissé ☆☆☆

This is a rising star in the Mâconnais, making remarkable Chardonnay both still and sparkling. The *crémant* is much more than lively, well-made fizz; it's a serious wine in its own right – elegant and aromatic, with great persistence of flavour.

Domaine Verret
89530 St-Bris-le-Vineux ☆☆
An accomplished Yonne grower using a little Sacy in the grape mix as well as Chardonnay and Pinot Noir.

A vital, dancing style of *crémant*, usually with two and a half years on lees. Also, excellent and fairly priced Chablis.

Cave de Viré
71260 Viré ☆
Like its neighbour, the Cave de Lugny, this is a sizeable producer of *crémant*. Sound quality, though its vintage-dated *cuvée* has a distinct oxidative style, which is an acquired taste.

Vitteaut-Alberti
71150 Rully ☆☆
A family business with eight and a half hectares of vineyard, supplying a quarter of its sparkling-wine needs; the rest of the grapes are bought in.

A serious qualitative approach involves hand riddling and around three years on lees. The 1995 *crémant* is elegant but evolved, and very good. It is listed at the fabled Lameloise restaurant in nearby Chagny.

CLAIRETTE AND CREMANT DE DIE
Clairette de Die was one of the first French wines made, reputedly drunk by the colonising Romans. The vineyards lie east of Valence (Rhône) in a valley of the Drôme, between Luc-en-Diois and Aouste-sur-Sye.

Production is essentially that of slightly sweet sparkling wine, dominated by the Muscat grape, which must make up at least 75 per cent of the grape mix, with the other 25 per cent provided by Clairette. An attractive, floral and grapey wine – a great match with fruit tarts or spicy Asian *cuisine*.

It is produced by the traditional *méthode dioise* – initially this process involves prolonged fermentations at very low temperatures, and with regular filtrations. The wine is then transferred to a stoppered bottle, where the fermentation continues and the resulting bubbles are imprisoned in the wine. In this way, the fresh fruity charms of the Muscat are preserved. There is no need to add *dosage de l'expédition*, as the wine already has a natural sweetness. An excellent local cooperative accounts for 80 per cent of production, with the remaining 20 per cent made by small growers.

By contrast, Crémant de Die is a Champagne-method sparkling-wine, made entirely from the Clairette grape, which is grown in the Drôme Valley. It was granted its own appellation in 1993.

Sud Est Appellations Clairette de Die
26150 Die ☆☆

Big is beautiful. This important, impeccably run cooperative, accounts for 80 per cent of the Clairette de Die production. The brand leader is the Tradition Clairdie, a unique, slightly sweet, and quite delicious sparkling wine, brimming with grapey-Muscat flavours. The wine is a little less fizzy than Champagne, with a reduced 3.5 atmospheres of pressure.

The Crémant de Die, Fontailly, is excellent. Made from a blend of several vintages back to 1991, and with four years on lees, it displays fine fruit-to-acid balance. The cooperative also makes a range of 12 still wines from the Rhône, including Crozes-Hermitage, Vacquéras and Châteauneuf-du-Pape.

Domaine de Magord
26150 Barsac ☆☆☆

The Vincent family's six-and-a-half-hectare *domaine* is the source of an exceptional, perfumed Clairette de Die Tradition made from pure Muscat grapes. Also, they make a fine, well-aged Crémant de Die of beautiful fruit and durable structure.

Georges Raspail
26340 Aurel ☆☆

A small producer making a very good Crémant de Die, with succulence and finesse in equal measure.

BLANQUETTE AND CREMANT DE LIMOUX

The Benedictine monks of St Hilaire at Limoux in the Languedoc are believed to have made a French sparking wine by the *méthode rurale* in 1531. Essentially the principle is to put incompletely fermented wine into a bottle to make it sparkle. Around 7.8 million bottles are produced each year in the Limouxin – the Caves du Sieur d'Arques being the largest producer. Permitted grapes are Mauzac (at least 90 per cent), Chenin Blanc and Chardonnay. In recent years the latter has replaced the Clairette grape in the interests of greater finesse.

In 1990, the new Crémant de Limoux appellation was created – made by the Champagne method, the permitted grapes are the same as for Blanquette, but the ratio of Mauzac to Chardonnay and Chenin Blanc is much smaller.

Personally, I prefer the clean, refined style of the new-style *crémant*s. The Limouxin also produces very good still white wines made with increasing amounts of Chardonnay.

Georges & Roger Antech
11300 Limoux ☆☆

Assured winemaking from the brothers Antech, who juggle Mauzac, Chenin Blanc and Chardonnay in the right ratio to produce racy, refined *crémant*s. Immaculate vineyard tending and modern cellar management.

Gerard Averseng
11300 La Digne d'Amont ☆☆☆☆

The champion grower and winemaker of top-flight Crémant de Limoux. A golden luxurious wine, aged for at least six years – all the hazelnut and gingerbread tones of full maturity are a delight. Tiny quantities.

Brouette Petit-Fils
11300 Limoux ☆☆

A respected producer making a very traditional Mauzac-dominated Blanquette.

Caves de Sieur d'Arques
11300 Limoux ☆☆

The leading producer of the Limouxin, with 500 hectares under vine, producing very reliable, floral and well-balanced Blanquette de Limoux under the vintage Diaphane label.

The 1994 Crémant de Limoux is even better, the finesse of Chardonnay and Chenin Blanc shows well. Also excellent prestige Grande Cuvée Renaissance. Brilliant still Limoux whites (Toques et Clochers – *see* the Glossary).

CREMANT DE BORDEAUX

Granted in 1990, the appellation Crémant de Bordeaux follows the same strict rules governing all French *crémants*.

The main grapes used are Sémillon, Sauvignon Blanc and Muscadelle. Of the three varieties the Sémillon, with such luscious yet refined character, should make some interesting sparkling wines in the future – it has an aptitude to develop those autolytic flavours that come after two to three years on lees. As yet, there are few memorable wines to recommend, but the potential is there. A little pink Crémant de Bordeaux is also made.

Brouette Petit-Fils
33170 Bourg ☆☆

Perhaps the most dependable of the Crémant de Bordeaux producers, with an admired vintage-dated Blanc de Blancs.

Les Cordeliers
33000 Bordeaux ☆☆

Established Bordeaux sparkling wine house, known for its special *cuvée* Blanc de Blancs – subtly aromatic with a Sémillon-led honeyed richness.

Société Bordelaise des Vins Mousseux
33200 Bordeaux ☆☆

As its name makes plain, the SBVM is a specialist sparkling wine producer. Very good Belair Cuvée Spéciale with a fine *mousse* and long Sauvignon Blanc flavours.

Union des Producteurs Baron d'Esprit
33420 Espiet ☆

A right-bank cooperative making pure, well-made *crémant* of marked Sémillon character – good quality-to-price ratio.

CREMANT DE JURA

The most recently created appellation of its type, Crémant de Jura came into force in 1995. The usual stringent rules governing the production of *crémant* apply.

Jura's native grape varieties – Poulsard and Pinot Noir for the black grapes; Chardonnay, Pinot Gris and Savagnin for white – are excellent raw materials for imaginative winemakers, who are seeking to create complex flavours in a sparkling wine. Great potential here.

Domaine Grand Freres
39230 Passenans ☆☆

The *domaine's* early trials with *crémant* have been very successful. This Chardonnay-led wine is powerful and would match a dish like *coulibiac* of salmon perfectly.

Claude Charbonnier
38570 Chillé ☆☆

A respected grower making a fine *crémant* from top-quality grapes grown in the 1.5-hectare Clos des Grives. Pure-toned primary fruit and model balance are the keynotes.

Château de L'Etoile
39560 L'Etoile ☆☆☆☆

Probably the most accomplished sparkling winemakers in the Jura, the Vandelles scale the heights with their vintage-dated *crémant* (excellent 1993 and 1995).

It is fresh, delicate and perfumed, but also complex, with evolved toast and honey flavours. Great wine.

Fruitiere Vinicole d'Arbois
39600 Arbois ☆☆

Important quality-conscious cooperative making an admired vintage-dated Blanc de Blancs – classy Chardonnay aromas of white flowers, and a poised harmony of flavours on the palate. Good ratio of quality to price.

Claude Rousselot-Pailley
39210 Lavigny ☆☆☆

A perfectionist grower-winemaker making 8,000 bottles a year of beautifully created Chardonnay-dominated *crémant*.

It is usually the product of a single year, with at least three years on lees. This sparkler is a vinous delight, and displays a finely judged balancing-act of freshness, vigour and buttery richness.

ST-PERAY

Opposite Valence, on the Ardèche side of the Rhône, lies the small commune of St-Péray. It has only 58 hectares of vineyards, planted predominantly with the Marsanne grape, which is in turn destined for the production of Champagne-method sparkling wine.

Traditionalists claim that it is one of the best sparkling wines of France. But frankly, it is hard to agree with this judgment in the late 1990s, particularly in light of the lively and elegant *crémants* from Alsace, Burgundy and the Jura that have emerged during the last 20 years.

Sparkling St-Péray is essentially a rustic wine, with a strong regional character, truly reflected in its style. It is definitely straw-like rather than lemony, and darker in colour than most modern sparkling wines. Traditionally it has an earthy flavour. But, in fairness, there is a newer style of St-Péray, made by up-to-the-minute techniques, which is lighter, brisker and more snappy. Generally speaking, this is not a sparkler that repays keeping to bring out latent complexities in the wine – after a few years, it quickly loses its vigour and fades.

Over the last half century, the numbers of merchants and growers making sparkling St-Péray has contracted drastically, and there are now only three principal growers making decent *mousseux* in the village, and a rather average-quality local cooperative.

Jean-Francois Chaboud
07130 St-Péray ☆☆

A leading grower in this area and producer of full-flavoured sparkling St-Péray from pure Marsanne.

With careful early bottling to achieve finer bubbles and preserve acidity, the *cuvées*, uniquely, are vintage dated. The wines are especially good with food – for instance ham, terrines and sausages.

Pierre Darona et fils
07130 St-Péray ☆

At their delightful farm outside the village, where they also grow apricots, the Darona family has been making sparkling St-Péray for half a century.

Nowadays it is a light clean and widely acceptable style, ideal served well chilled as an *apéritif*.

Jean-Louis Thiers
07130 St-Péray ☆☆

The son of a St-Péray grower, Jean-Louis Thiers is a very competent modern winemaker who studied in Beaune and now produces highly creditable St-Péray Mousseux in a racy, fresh, non-oxidative style.

Germany

Sekt, or sparkling wine manufactured in Germany, is big business. The Germans drink huge quantities of sekt every year, enabling the largest sparkling wine companies to achieve sales figures for their biggest brands that run in to the tens of millions.

Their success has been founded upon the simple formula of making sparkling wine available at rock bottom prices. In order to achieve this they have sacrificed the quality on the altar of commerce. It is hard to believe, but at the turn of the century brands of German sparkling wine such as Henkell Trocken and Kupferberg Gold were as expensive and highly esteemed as good Champagne!

Today, most of the big-selling sekt brands are made from the cheapest foreign base wine available, usually from Southern Italy. These are cleaned up, then tank fermented as rapidly and cost effectively as possible. Sadly, none of these products are likely to interest anyone who is used to drinking well-made Méthode-Champenoise sparkling wines.

Thankfully, however, there are also smaller sparkling wine companies who buy in their base wines from France or Germany and turn out a good quality product for a fair price. The very best of these wines are made by the Méthode Champenoise and are superior to many cheap Champagnes. Unfortunately they are not widely exported and therefore little-known internationally.

At the top of the quality pyramid are limited-production sparkling wines produced by Germany's top wine estates. These are made either from Riesling or the Pinot family of grapes. Examples from the more southerly Pfalz and Baden regions have a similar amount of body and a comparable balance to Champagne, whilst those from the northerly Mosel-Saar-Ruwer, Nahe and Rheingau regions are generally lighter and crisper. The quality ranges from sekts that taste like sparkling mineral water with an addition of alcohol, up to a handful of first-class sparkling wines.

Given the climate and geology of Germany's wine-growing regions, the potential for making great sparkling wines is undoubtedly present. If very few producers have realised this so far, then it is the attitude of German consumers which is the problem. They seem happy to accept sekts at prices of up to DMten per bottle on the shelf; but above this price and the word Champagne has to appear on the label. In order to be commercially viable, a great sparkling wine would have to be significantly more expensive than this.

Weingut Carl Adelseck
55424 Münster-Sarmsheim Nahe ☆☆

Unusually this small estate is better known for its sparkling wines than the still ones. These sparklers may be a touch on the sweet side; but Adekseck Juwel Trocken is full of fruit and impeccably made. This Riesling sekt should be drunk on its release for its vibrant, youthful flavours.

Weingut Karl Kurt Bamberger & Sohn
55566 Meddersheim Nahe ☆☆

This father and son team are the dark horses of the German sparkling wine scene. Since the release of their 1993 vintage sparkling wines, they have been showered with praise by the German wine press, and rightly so.

These are model sparkling wines in the Germanic style – with the emphasis on forthright fruit aromas underlayed by a streak of biscuity, yeasty notes. Best of the range is the juicy and elegant Riesling Trocken.

Weingut Hans Barth
65347 Hattenheim Rheingau ☆☆

Norbert Barth makes everything from Spätburgunder (Pinot Noir) reds to Riesling Eiswein at his 11-hectare estate, but his sekt puts them in the shade.

Best of all is the superb Blanc de Noir Ultra, launched at the begining of the 1990s – one of the most sophisticated and refined sparkling wines made in all of Germany. His Riesling sekts are consistently good too, but do not quite scale to these heights.

Weingut Bergdolt
67435 Duttweiler Pfalz ☆☆☆

The modest Rainer Bergdolt not only produces Germany's best dry Weissburgunder (Pinot Blanc), excellent barrel-fermented Chardonnay, impressive Spätburgunder reds, and good Rieslings at his 18-hectare estate, he is also one of the nation's leading sekt producers.

Perhaps he is still lacking one "star" product that could write headlines, but the consistent high quality across his range is unsurpassed.

The vintage-dated Weissburgunder Extra Brut displays excellent harmony in spite of the complete lack of *dosage,* while posessing a nutty, biscuity character. Further still, the rich Spätburgunder Blanc de Noirs Brut could easily pass for an old-fashioned-style Champagne. The Riesling Brut is an ample style for a sparkler made from this grape – with an excellent balance of fruit and acidity underscored by a restrained yeastiness.

Weingut Georg Breuer
65385 Rüdesheim Rhiengau ☆☆

This leading Rheingau estate is best known for making some of the nation's finest dry Rieslings from its extensive holdings in the top vineyard sites of Rüdesheim and Rauenthal. Owner

Bernhard Breuer tirelessly campaigns for their classification as Erster Gewächse (Grands Crus). His sekts are impressive – the vintage-dated GB Riesling Brut and GB Weissburgunder Brut are both substantial, full of fruit and pleasantly dry.

The rich and complex Georg Breuer Brut is a blend of Riesling, Weissburgunder, Grauburgunder, and Spätburgunder. It is barrel fermented and spends about five years on lees, and is most impressive.

Deinhard
56068 Koblenz ☆

Late in 1997 the Wegeler family sold its controlling interest in the family company to sekt business giants Henkell-Söhnlein. As yet it is difficult to see what effect this will have upon Deinhard's range of cheap and modestly priced sekts.

At present only the Lila can be recommended. It is made primarily from Riesling base wines from the Mittelrhein, and is a well-made, typical German sekt.

Schlossgut Diel
55452 Burg Layen Nahe ☆☆

This is a leading Nahe estate, and concentrates on classic-style Riesling-Kabinett and -Spätlese wines with natural sweetness, plus barrel-fermented dry wines from the Pinot family of grapes.

But, Armin Diel's vintage-dated Méthode Champenois Riesling Extra Trocken sekt is impressive, and shows more mature leesy character than most products of this type.

Geldermann
79206 Breisach ☆☆

This is perhaps Germany's leading *sektkellerei* (the equivalent of a *négociant-manipulant* in Champagne).

The principal product – Geldermann Brut – is a blend of Chardonnay and Chenin Blanc from the Loire, primarily from the Château de L'Aulée estate. The result is a bready, spicy bouquet and a medium-bodied wine with fine mousse.

This wine can hardly be considered typical of a German sekt, but both in quality and style it can bear comparison with lighter Champagnes.

Graeger
65239 Hochheim ☆

A small sekt company which is situated in the Rheingau, and specialises in Riesling sekt – made from base wines which are sourced in that region.

These are light and aromatic styles, with pronounced peachy notes. And they are very likely to be amongst the best modestly priced, commercially available sekts made from German base wines.

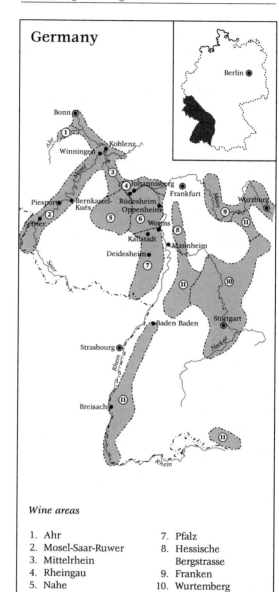

Germany

Wine areas

1. Ahr
2. Mosel-Saar-Ruwer
3. Mittelrhein
4. Rheingau
5. Nahe
6. Rheinhessen
7. Pfalz
8. Hessische Bergstrasse
9. Franken
10. Wurtemberg
11. Baden

Weingut Reinhold Haart
54498 Piesport Mosel ☆☆

Theo Haart has almost single-handedly put Piesport back on the map as a producer of great Mosel-Riesling wines.

His interest in sparkling wine production dates back to the late 1980s, and from the beginning he set himself the same high standards as with his still wines. With subtle fruit aromas and an elegant harmony as his goal, he developed a distinctive style based on wines with moderate acidity and no more than two years lees ageing.

His Riesling Brut is very dry, having only a minimal *dosage*; the excellent Riesling Trocken is juicy and polished without being in any way too sweet.

Henkell-Söhnlein (with Fürst von Metternich)
65201 Wiesbaden-Schierstein ☆

Most of this sparkling wine giant's production consists of extremely commercial brands, positioned at the lower end of the price scale. The hugely successful Henkell Trocken is, to take one example, hardly an advertisement for the abilities of the nation's sparkling winemakers.

However, the Fürst von Metternich range is another matter. These are made exclusively from Rheingau-Riesling base-wines and are of consistently good quality. They always show a good balance of fruity, yeasty character – the vintage Brut has the most depth and impressive balance.

Weingut Heymann-Löwenstein
56333 Winningen Mosel ☆☆

Reinhard Löwenstein not only makes dry Mosel-Riesling wines that are unusually full and ripe, he also makes sekt that is equally unusual for its region.

The vintage-dated Riesling Extra Brut is the most successful *sans-dosage* sparkling wine in the Mosel, with full apple character and a crisp, remarkably harmonious finish.

Weingut Bernhard Huber
79364 Malterdingen Baden ☆☆☆

Bernhard Huber is the new winemaking star of the Baden region. He first attracted attention with his Spätburgunder red wines, which are arguably Germany's finest reds. But his barrel-fermented Chardonnay, from old vines, has also won several blind tastings.

His sekts deserve to be every bit as well known and highly regarded as his still wines, since they are clearly the finest in his region. The Pinot Brut *rosé* (100% Pinot Noir) is first class, its cherry and *brioche* bouquet leads to a full-bodied *rosé* that is impeccably balanced. The Pinot Brut (a blend of the white Pinot grapes) with aromas of pear and vanilla, and a full, very clean flavour, is no less impressive.

Weingut Johannishof
65366 Johannisberg Rheingau ☆☆☆
Hans Hermann Eser's Kabinett Brut may be one of the most expensive Riesling sekts in Germany; but it is also, more importantly, frequently the very best.

The 1990 vintage was superb, striking exactly the right balance between fine and peachy Riesling fruit, and the mature nutty, biscuity character.

The 1994 is presently (in 1998) a bit too young, but is not far behind in quality. It is simultaneously sleek and concentrated. These sekts have a classical elegance rarely found in German sparkling wines.

Weingut Koehler-Ruprecht
67169 Kallstadt Pfalz ☆☆☆
For those with a taste for big, rich sparkling wines – in the style of Bollinger or Krug – the best Germany has to offer is unquestionably Bernd Philippi's extraordinary Philippi Pinot Blanc Brut.

This blockbuster sparkler is packed with nutty mature flavours, and has exactly the right amount of acidity to support its very full body. The entire range of sekts from Riesling and the Pinot family of grapes is excellent, plus the development of the range is still underway.

Philippi's aim is to bring them up to the same spectacular standard as his great dry Rieslings and Spätburgunder reds – he is not far from reaching this goal.

WG Königsschaffhausen
79346 Königschaffhausen Baden ☆☆
This model cooperative produces the full range of dry-white and red wines typical for the Kaiserstuhl area, and enjoys a good reputation for them in Germany.

Sadly, one of its most interesting and successful wines – a speciality and very good vintage-dated Weissburgunder Brut – remains almost completely unknown. This style is full, biscuity and nutty, and always benefits from at least three years on lees.

Weingut Dr Loosen
54470 Bernkastel Mosel ☆☆☆
This is the Mosel's leading wine estate, and produces not only the region's most concentrated Riesling wines, but also a small quantity of remarkable Riesling sekt.

Inspired by Bollinger RD, Ernst Loosen leaves his vintage-dated Riesling Brut almost ten years on lees, giving it a complexity and depth that you rarely find in German sparkling wines. This also masks the commonly high acidity, giving a style that is quite different from the tartness typical of Mosel Riesling sekt.

Sektgut Menger-Krug
55239 Gau-Ordenheim Rheinhessen ☆☆

This double estate, with vineyards in Rheinhessen and in the Pfalz, is one of Germany's most consistent and reliable producers of quality sekt.

The husband and wife team Klaus and Regina Menger makes a range of well-crafted modern-style sparkling wines which are fresh, clean, balanced and on the dry side. Most successful is the Weissburgunder-dominated Pinot Cuvée.

Schloss Münzingen (inc Graf von Kageneck)
79206 Breisach Baden ☆

In spite of the mention of castles and an aristocratic name printed on the label, this is the sparkling wine arm of the Badische Winzerkeller, Baden's giant cooperative.

Whilst its varietal sekts, from Riesling and the Pinot family, are not the most sophisticated in the region, they have plenty of character and are of consistently solid quality.

Schloss Neuweier
76534 Neuweier Baden ☆☆

Unusually for Baden, this estate specialises in dry Riesling wines. The Riesling Brut sekt may not be up to the high standard of the best still wines, but is full of peach and melon fruit and crisp enough to balance the rather generous *dosage*.

Weingut Ratzenberger
55422 Bacharach Mittelrhein ☆☆

The Mittelrhein region is pre-destined for the production of Riesling sekt, as its Riesling wines combine a racy acidity with the ideal amount of body for their base wines. Sadly, few of the region's growers have successfuly turned this potential into first-class products.

Jochen Ratzenberger's vintage-dated Riesling Brut stands out from most in this region due to its crisp leanness and bright Riesling flavours.

Reh-Gruppe (including Feist)
54290 Trier ☆

Another of Germany's sparkling wine giants; best known for the Faber range of very cheap, very commercial sekts.

Far better is the Feist Riesling – an attractive and fruity aromatic sparkler.

Weingut Schloss Reinhartshausen
65346 Erbach Rheingau ☆☆☆

This 100-hectare estate is rightly renowned for producing some of the finest wines in the Rheingau.

In the sparkling wine field it also offers some superb products – most notably the extremely elegant and nutty

Weissburgunder Brut – very similar in style to a good Blanc de Blancs Champagne. The clean, racy Riesling sekts are excellent examples of classical German-style sparkling wines. They benefit from a year or two of bottle ageing after release.

Weingut Selbach-Oster
54492 Zeltingen Mosel ☆☆

Zeltingen may not be as famous as next door Wehlen, but in the hands of a talented winemaker like Johannes Selbach its vineyards can reward both still and sparkling wines as fine as those of its neighbour.

The Riesling Brut is a model sparkling Mosel wine – clean, fruity and vigorous; without the hard acidity that so often mars these products.

Schloss Vaux
65346 Eltville ☆☆

A small, very traditional sparkling wine house making some very good sekt from base wines purchased from some of the Rheingau's leading estates.

Some of these may be a little too dry or acidic for those used to good Champagne; but the winemaking is impeccable. The result is pure flavour, with the subtle underscoring of the wine's fruity and yeasty elements.

Weingut Dr. Heinz Wagner
54439 Saarburg Saar ☆☆☆

There could hardly be a better introduction to quality sekt than Heinz Wagner's Riesling Brut, a minor masterpiece of sparkling winemaking in the classic German style. In spite of a good two years on lees, it is still the fine Riesling fruit aromas which dominate the subtle bouquet.

Whilst it may not be able to match a top Champagne for weight and body on the palate, it is certainly equal in elegance. The high acidity content is also effortlessly integrated. Perhaps this should be no surprise since the ancestors of shy, winemaking-genius Heinz Wagner were the leading producers of Saar sekt until the 1920s.

Weingut Wilhelmshof
76833 Siebeldingen Pfalz ☆☆

Herberth Roth's declared goal is to match the winemakers of Champagne, which might seem rather arrogant were it not for the consistently high quality of his sekts.

The most successful wine in his range – the vintage-dated Blanc de Noirs – already achieves this goal. It is full bodied, with a fine raspberry and toast character, and has near-perfect balance. His other sekts, from the Riesling and Pinot family, are not far behind – all have a good balance of fruit and lees character, plus well-judged *dosage*.

Italy

Three thousand years ago, the colonising Greeks called Italy "Oenotria" – the land of wine. An apt description of a country dominated by hills and mountains, and thus ideal for the cultivation of the vine.

In most years Italy makes about six billion bottles of wine from a myriad of grape varieties, usurping France's position as the number one wine producer in the world. Since the early 1970s, Italian wine has undergone a *renaissance*, with quality improving across the spectrum from classic powerful reds to light, racy whites.

Dry sparkling wine has been one of the great growth areas of northern Italy, particularly in Lombardy and Piedmont, where *metodo classico* wines are now offering serious alternatives to Champagne. In 1996, several prominent sparkling wine producers in the north of Italy adopted the collective trading name "Talento" in an attempt to create a recognisable interregional appellation.

PIEDMONT

Southeast of Turin, the town of Canelli in the province of Asti is the capital of Italy's best-known sparkling wine. Sparkling Asti or Asti Spumante (as it is more commonly recognised) is made from the Moscato di Canelli grape, grown in a vast zone of 40,000 hectares in the districts of southern Monferrato and the eastern Langhe hills.

The total production each year is some 77 million litres (17 million gallons), which makes Asti the second-biggest sparkling wine globally after Champagne. Unsurprisingly, Asti Spumante is mainly produced by large companies with the technology to handle the delicate Moscato grape on an industrial scale. Long, cool fermentations are conducted in closed tanks to preserve the vibrant fruit and a little residual sugar. The finished wines are slightly sweet, moderately alcoholic (up to nine per cent) and fully sparkling.

The quality has improved markedly in recent years, thanks to the stringent controls specified in the Asti DOCG rules. The superior Moscato d'Asti is a fashionable wine in the restaurants of Turin. These are less fizzy and lower in alcohol (five to six per cent) than Asti Spumante. The best sparking Moscato comes from small *vignaioli* (growers) higher in the Langhe hills towards Alba. The intensity of this grape's aromas is captivating, and the wine's low strength makes it a wonderfully refreshing drink with a ripe peach on a summer's day.

The Freisa grape produces distinctive, cherry-hued *frizzante* (slightly sparkling) in Piedmont. A drier version from a top grower like Aldo Vayra in Barolo can delight with its raspberry-like fruit. Forget all your prejudices about fizzy red wine and enjoy!

Italy

Wine areas

1. Valle d'Aosta
2. **Piedmont**
3. **Lombardy**
4. Liguria
5. Emilia Romagna
6. Veneto
7. Friuli–
   Venezia Giulia
8. **Trentino–**
   Alto Adige

Bava

Cocconato Asti ☆☆☆

A close-knit family business, by the railway station. Exporters of excellent Piedmontese red varietals – including superb, well-aged Barberas and the intriguing Ruchè di Castagnole Monferrato. The sparkling wines are also worth a look, particularly the pure-flavoured Moscato and Freisa d'Asti.

Caudrina Dogliotti

Çastiglione Cuneo ☆☆☆

Top-flight producers of Moscato d'Asti under La Caudrina and La Galeisa labels.

Michele Chiarlo

Calamandrana Asti ☆☆

The wide range of wines – red and white, still and sparkling – includes sound Moscato (Rocca della Rionda) and Asti Spumante. Plus, the impressive Granduca Brut *metodo classico*.

Cinzano

Torino ☆☆

Internationally known as a vermouth producer, this very old firm also produces large amounts of creditable Asti Spumante

by the Champagne and Charmat methods. The Cinzano *non dose* is the best sparkler.

Giuseppe Contratto
Canelli Asti ☆☆☆

Immaculate quality across the board at this traditionalist firm, with excellent sparkling Moscato and Asti, and exceptional Brut Riserva *metodo classico*.

Fontanafredda
Serralunga d'Alba Cuneo ☆☆☆

A historic house, founded by the royal house of Savoy, now has Livia Testa as its winemaker. A classic Alba range, including an elegant Asti Spumante and top-flight *metodo classico* Contessa Rose Brut and *rosé*, plus the Gattinera Brut.

Gancia
Canelli Asti ☆☆

One of the founders of the Asti sparkling wine industry in the 1860s; this family owned firm remains a force to be reckoned with. The classically made Vallarino Gancia Gran Crémant Riserva is a wine of subtle class, while the tank method Pinot di Pinot is buoyantly fruity – a party wine.

Bruno Giacosa
Neive Cuneo ☆☆☆☆

Bruno Giacosa is a guardian of tradition, and makes a range of outstanding Barbaresco and Barolo.

His Spumante Classico Extra Brut is also exceptional – as good as any sparkling wine outside Champagne, and better than much within it. The fine, dry frizzante Freisa d'Asti is also recommended.

Martini & Rossi
Torino ☆☆to☆☆☆

Everyone knows the Martini vermouths, but this celebrated firm also makes large amounts of sparkling wine at Santa Stephano Belbo.

Two recommendations include the sparkling Riesling, based on bought-in grapes from Oltrepò Pavese; and the very classy Spumante Classico (Riserva Montelera Brut).

Marco Negri
Costigliole d'Asti Asti ☆☆☆☆

Possibly considered the greatest producer of Moscato d'Asti, Marco Negri consistently makes a wine of exquisite fragrance and perfect balance. Well worth a try.

Riccadonna
Canelli Asti ☆☆

Established in the early 1920s, Riccadonna is now one of the giants of the Asti industry. The quality across the range is sound but unexciting.

Its Asti Spumante is sweeter than most, and the Charmat-method President Brut is rather one-dimensional. The best *cuvées* are the *metodo classico* Conte Balduino Extra Brut and the Riserva Privata Angelo Riccadonna.

Servetti
Cassine Alessandria ☆☆

A respected producer of the Chiriera Moscato d'Asti and the interesting red, strawberry-flavoured, *frizzante* Brachetto d'Acqui (DOCG in 1996).

I Vignaioli di Santo Stefano
Santo Stefano Belbo Cuneo ☆☆☆

This is a progressive, modern-minded operation making an impressive Moscato d'Asti.

Gianni Voerzio
La Morra Cuneo ☆☆☆

A great red winemaker (especially his Barolos La Serra and Brunate), and there is no slouching with the *frizzante* either in his fine Vignasergente Moscato d'Asti.

G D Vajra
Barolo Cuneo ☆☆☆☆

In his modern, stain-glass-windowed winery, with views to the Alps, the softly spoken and cultivated Aldo Vajra makes great Barolo as subtle as the man himself.

From the Langhe DOC, he also produces the best *frizzante* Freisa available – it is packed with strawberry fruitiness, but is dry and well balanced.

LOMBARDY

Centred on the great city of Milan, Lombardy is the most densely populated and industrialised region of Italy, with one of the highest standards of living in Europe. The Lombardians do not have a distinctive wine culture in the way that the Tuscans or the Piedmontese do. But, the Milanese in particular are very discerning *gastronomes* and have provided an excellent local market, and much of the capital, for the outstanding sparkling (and still) wines now coming out of Franciacorta – the region's most dynamic wine zone.

To the west of Brescia by the shores of Lake Isea, Franciacorta is, in Burton Anderson's words, "a miniature Champagne". Being influenced by a group of wealthy and perfectionist estate owners, notably Ca'del Bosco (qv), this is certainly the most strictly controlled DOCG of any sparkling wine in Italy.

Its provisions make even the rigorous Champenois look lax by comparison. The youngest wine in the *cuvée* must be aged for 25 months, including at least 18 months in bottle after the *prise de mousse*. The minimum ageing period for a vintage wine is just over three years. Like Champagne, only the place name Franciacorta appears on the label – terms like *metodo classico* or *metodo tradizionale* are forbidden. The permitted grapes for use in its production are Chardonnay, Pinot Bianco and Pinot Nero (Noir), and yields are restricted to 65 hl/ha.

Chardonnay-dominated blends are increasingly popular and there are some impressive Blanc de Blancs. Franciacorta *rosé* must contain at least 15 per cent Pinot Nero. The Franciacorta equivalent of a *crémant*-style Champagne (one that is less than fully sparkling) has to be made only from white grapes and can be recognised by the trade-name Sáten.

The preferred style of wine is overwhelmingly Brut and there is quite a number of *cuvées* within this category that have no *dosage* added and may be termed *pas dose*, extra brut, Brut Zéro etc.

The total production entitled to the DOCG is three million bottles a year, and the quality of the best estates – Ca'del Bosco, Bellavista and Cavalleri – is high, with prices to match. The local, excellent still wines have their own new DOC – Terre di Franciacorta.

Guido Berlucchi
Borgonato di Cortefranca Brescia ☆☆
Founded by the Berlucchi family in the 1960s, this is the largest producer of *metodo classico* sparkling wines in Italy, some 400,000 cases a year.

Wine *supremo* Franco Zillani oversees the production of five *cuvées*: with Imperial Berlucchi Brut, Brut Millesimato, Grand Crémant, *pas dose*, and Max Rosé. Though these are made in Franciacorta, the wines are not classified as DOCG, but are of sound quality.

Bellavista
Erbusco Brescia ☆☆☆☆
Both owner Vittorio Moretti and winemaker Mattia Vezzola produce exceptional Franciacorta across a range of classic sparkling wines.

Their greatest offerings are probably the 100-per-cent Chardonnay Gran Cuvée Millesimato and the Riserva Vittoria Moretti – world-class wines of supreme elegance, and long mature flavours.

Ca' del Bosco
Erbusco Brescia ☆☆☆☆
This house is the leading Franciacorta estate, and run with perfectionism by the approachable and informative Maurizio Zanelli. The sparkling wines are peerless, with the blends ranging from Brut, *crémant*, *rosé*, and *dosage zero* to the Brut Millesimato (great 1980) and the barrel-fermented Cuvée Anna Maria Clemente.

Excellent still wines include an exceptional Chardonnay and a poised and stylish Pinero (Pinot Nero).

Castelfaglia
Cassargo San Martino Brescia ☆☆
A lesser-known producer of fine DOCG Franciacorta.

Uberti
Erbusco Brescia ☆☆☆
An excellent maker of DOCG Franciacorta – fine Francesco 1 Brut and *pas dose*. Also, a very good Cabernet Sauvignon called Rosso dei Frati Priori.

TRENTINO–ALTO ADIGE
Dominated by the peaks of the Dolomites, these are Italy's most northern regions, with progressively Germanic influences the closer you come to the Brenner Pass and Austrian border. These areas are important producers of sparkling wines both by the Charmat and *classico* methods. In the latter category the best sparklers, such as Spagnolli's Trento Brut Classico (qv) are made from Chardonnay and

Pinot Nero. They appear under Alto Adige DOC Spumante and Trento DOC, but a significant number are not classified.

Ca'Vit (Cantina Viticoltori Trento)
Trento ☆☆☆

This huge cooperative with 4,000 member growers makes three quarters of all the wine produced in the Trento province. One of winemaker, Giacinto Giacomino's, best bargains is the Charmat-method Gran Spumante Ca'Vit Brut.

The fine Trento Brut Riserva Graal – a Pinot Noir and Chardonnay – is highly recommended.

Concilio
Volano Trento ☆☆☆

A rejuventated company, founded in 1972 by the merger of two older wineries. They are best known for their first-class Merlot (Novaline) and excellent Brut di Concilio *tradizione*.

Equipe Trentina Spumante
Messalombardo Trento ☆☆☆

A highly regarded Spumante producer, known particularly for its racy and fine Trento Brut Equipe 5.

Kettmeir
Caldaro Bolzano ☆☆

One of the largest firms in the Alto Aldige, now owned by Santa Margherita in Veneto. A full range of varietals (good Merlot Siebeneich) and two sparklers – the Grand Cuvée Brut and the Gran Spumante Rosé.

Ferrari-Fratelli
Lunelli Trento ☆☆☆*to*☆☆☆☆

This family firm was founded in 1902, and has a long-standing reputation for exceptional *metodo classico* sparkling wines. Now owned and managed by the Lunelli brothers, one of whom, Mauro, is the winemaker.

They produce around one million bottles a year. And of this number, in particular, the stunning ☆☆☆☆ Guilio Ferrari Riserva del Fondatore holds great finesse and distinction; also the excellent, bone-dry Maximum Brut.

Fratelli Pisoni
Pergolese Sarche Trento ☆☆

A fine Trento-*metodo-classico* Brut and a delicious Vin Santo dessert wine are recommended.

Schloss/Castel Schwanburg
Merano Bolzano ☆☆

An old and distinguished estate making DOC Alto Adige and *spumante* wines.

Armando Simoncelli
Navicello di Rovereto Trento ☆☆☆

This is a top grower, making the elegant and fine-drawn Simoncelli Brut Trento Classico; and a splendid Marzemino, among the DOC reds.

G Spagnolli
Aldeno Trento ☆☆☆☆

Francesco Spagnolli makes the outstanding Trento DOC Spagnolli Brut, a blend of Chardonnay and Pinot Nero, and one of Italy's greatest sparkling wines. A great partner to the local blue trout, cooked in a little of Spagnolli's own Brut.

Vivaldi
Meltina Bolzano ☆☆☆

Joseph Reiterer makes excellent *tradizionale* Brut and Extra Brut – the best of the sparklers from Alto Adige.

VENETO

The Veneto, Venice's wine region, is the most productive vineyard of northern Italy. Two thirds of the region is on the flatlands, notably in the valley of the River Po. Yet, all the best wines are grown on the first tentative foothills of the Alps, or in elevated outcrops extending east from Lake Garda to the River Piave.

The latter is the home of Prosecco, the lightly bubbling wine that is the most popular sparkler in Italy after Asti. This wine takes its name from the Prosecco grape, grown in the lovely hills north of the Piave, between Conegliano and Valdobbiadene. Although the wine may be made still, much of it is made sparkling by the Charmat method. Production is now some 2.2 million cases a year; a tiny fraction of this total may be labelled "Cartizze" – a selection of superior Prosecco, from grapes grown in a delimited zone near Valdobbiadene. In reality the production of "Cartizze" greatly exceeds the legal limit (some 800,000 bottles).

The best Prosecco has a fruity aroma and is nicely rounded on the palate, but with an aftertaste of bitter almonds that checks any tendency to blandness. It is ideal as an *apéritif* and a very good match with shellfish taken straight from the Adriatic.

Carpene Malvolti
Conegliano Treviso ☆☆

This firm was founded in the late 1860s, and was one of the first to make sparkling wines using the Champagne method, in the Veneto region.

It is best known today for the admired DOC Prosecco di Conegliano. The *metodo classico* Carpene Mavolti Brut is also recommended.

Collalto
Susegana Treviso ☆☆☆

This up and coming estate leads with an excellent DOC Prosecco di Conegliano, backed by a raft of interesting varietal wines such as Piave Chardonnay, and the very rare red Wildbacher.

Conte Loredan-Gasparini
Volpage del Montello Treviso ☆☆☆

Famed for their Venegazzù red wines of noble lineage, this house also makes a fine traditional-method Brut *spumante*, in a classic 60 per cent Chardonnay, 40 per cent Pinot Nero mix.

It is aged for at least 36 months on lees, and shows excellent fruit and autolytic flavours.

Nino Franco
Valdobbiadene Treviso ☆☆☆

A respected Prosecco producer, with fine hillside sites that are entitled to the superior "Cartizze" appellation. This top wine is dry, subtle, and refined.

The family also make an old-style sweet bubbly, which goes well with desserts.

Opere Trevigiani
Crocetta del Montella Treviso ☆☆

Well-regarded makers of both DOC Prosecco and a classic-method *spumante* Opere.

Santa Margherita
Portogruaro Veneto ☆☆☆

An important and enlightened wine house, owned by the Mazotto family, with interests that extend beyond the production of its own very-good sparkling wines.

The company has a share in, and handles the marketing of, Ca'del Bosco's Franciacorta. They also own Kettmeir in the Alto Adige (qv), as well as two Chianti estates in Tuscany.

Zandeto
Conegliano Treviso ☆☆☆☆

Pino and Fabio Zandetto make superb Prosecco and Cartizze, unmatched for their fragrance, elegance, and purity of fruit.

Perfect wines to drink by the Venice Lagoon with spider crab, dressed with oil and lemon.

Zonin
Gamberalla Vincenza ☆☆to☆☆☆

A giant family owned company, with a good eye for quality and a hungry urge for acquisitions. They offer a broad range of wines, including sound *spumante*. Also other interests in Piedmont, Lombardy, Friuli, Tuscany and Sicily.

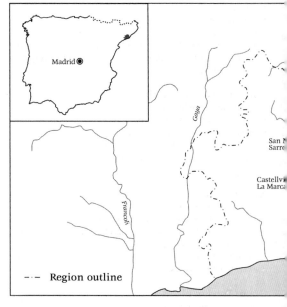

Madrid ●

San ℕ
Sarr

Castellví
La Marca

Gaia

Francoli

-·- **Region outline**

Spain

In 1872 Don José Raventós returned from Champagne to his
home town of San Sadurní de Noya (Sant Sadurní d'Anoia),
the capital of Catalonia. Here in the cellars of his family firm,
Cordorníu, he made the first bottles of Spanish sparkling
wine by the *méthode champenoise*.

Progress was impeded by the invasion of the *phylloxera
vastratix* aphid, which was first reported in Catalonia in 1881.
Every affected red-wine variety had to be pulled up and the
vineyards replanted with indigenous, grafted white varieties.
The *phylloxera* outbreak was a blessing in disguise, for it
encouraged the local Catalan firms, such as Cordorníu and its
chief rival Freixenet (founded 1889), to specialise in sparkling
wines and become very prosperous.

In the 1990s, both Cordorníu and Freixenet are among
the most important firms in this field, with satellites in
California and, in the case of Freixenet, in Champagne itself
(*see* Henri Abelé).

The Spanish have been quick to give their sparkling wines
a strong identity, quite distinct from that of Champagne. In
1970, they started using the simple, easy-to-pronounce word
"cava" in place of the problematic "Champagna". The litigious
Champenois were appeased and an instantly recognisable
generic name was born. Since 1986, cava has been awarded
its DO appellation, and may be made in 155 municipalities in

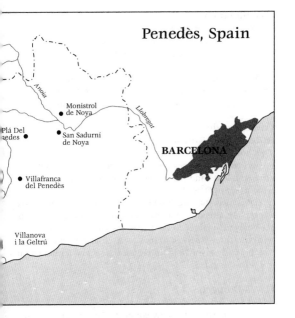

Penedès, Spain

Anoia

Plá Del edes ●

Monistrol de Noya ●

● San Sadurní de Noya

Llobregat

BARCELONA

● Villafranca del Penedès

Villanova i la Geltrú

eight provinces across northern Spain. In reality, 95 per cent of all cava is produced in Catalonia.

Traditionally the wines have been made from three Spanish grapes. The workhorse, and rather bland, Macabeo is the most productive, accounting for up to 50 per cent of a typical cava blend. The Xarel-lo, also a prolific cropper, imparts a burnt-earth aroma to cava which you either love or hate. The Parellada, particularly when grown at higher altitudes, is the classiest of the three grapes, bringing the wines some much needed finesse.

Chardonnay is now also being introduced to the cava blend, particularly by the big houses. As for the winemaking, cava follows the principles of the traditional method, though the rules of the DO are in some respects less demanding than those of the Champagne AOC. Cava wine must spend at least nine months in bottle after the *prise de mousse* (16 months for Champagne), plus the maximum yield of 100 hectolitres per hectare is higher than Champagne's.

The total annual production of cava is about 100 million litres a year. Like all Spanish wine, cava has benefited in recent years from the technology of cool fermentation in stainless steel tanks; and automatic-riddling-machines called *girasols* are also commonly found. At half the price of a middling Champagne, cava has made great inroads into the sparkling wine market in Britain.

Castellblanch
08770 San Sadurní de Noya ☆☆

Owned by Freixenet since the mid-1980s, this is a large firm which produces only cava wines, both from bought-in grapes and its own sizeable vineyards.

Much of the range is made in an off-dry style, though the Brut Zero is a notch up in quality – striking a good balance between clean fruit and a nice touch of autolytic maturity.

Cava Chandon
08739 Subirats Barcelona ☆☆to☆☆☆

This house – Moët & Chandon's sparkling wine venture in Spain – is now ten years old and benefits greatly from the *virtuoso* talents and regular advice of Richard Geoffroy, the winemaker of Dom Pérignon.

The cavas that are produced in the new state-of-the-art winery are already good and will surely improve further as the vineyard, planted in 1988, matures. Chardonnay, together with the three Spanish grapes, is used also in the blends. The Brut – aged for 24 months after the second fermentation – is recommended.

Cavas Domecq
08770 San Sadurní de Noya ☆☆☆

The giant sherry and brandy company, Domecq, has its own cava subsidiary in Catalonia. The Brut is admired for its complex flavours and balance and there is a *rosé* version based on the Garnacha grape. Lembey is a second label.

Cavas Hill
08734 Moja ☆☆☆

One of the oldest cava houses, dating back to 1887, Cavas Hill built a new winery in 1990 to allow for a big increase in production. Both still and sparkling wines are made, in part sourced from the firm's 50 hectares of vines.

The very-dry Brutissimo is one of the best cavas on the market – clean as a whistle but with a complexity of flavour that only comes from extended ageing in bottle.

Cavas Ferret
08770 San Sadurní de Noya ☆☆☆

A small, quality-conscious *bodega*, modernised in the mid-1980s, which makes a genuinely refined dry Brut with a high percentage of Parellada grapes.

Codorníu
08770 San Sadurní de Noya ☆☆to☆☆☆

A venerable Penedès firm dating back to the 16th century, Codorníu is now a colossus of the cava industry, and produces around 45-million bottles of sparkling wine a year.

Three quarters of its grape needs come from a wide network of growers and a consistent house style relies strongly on the use of older reserve wines.

The strong card of the best-selling Brut Classico is reliability rather than character. But, the top-of-the-range, Jaime de Cordorníu 1551, is made from a classic mix of Chardonnay and Pinot Noir (a first in Penedès), and tastes remarkably like good Champagne.

The house was built by a pupil of Gaudi and has a wine museum with a beautiful park (*see also* Codorníu Napa).

Conde de Caralt
08770 San Sadurní de Noya ☆☆
In the same stable as Segura Viudas, and owned by Freixenet, this *bodega* produces good-value and sound cava, with typical burnt-earth flavours of the Xarel-lo grape. The Brut Nature is the best *cuvée*.

Freixenet
08770 San Sadurní de Noya ☆☆☆
The Ferrer family owns this huge cava firm and has expanded its operations on a global scale, acquiring the Champagne house of Henri Abelé in 1985, and launching a sparkling wine operation in California – Gloria Ferrer (qv) – the following year.

Big can be beautiful, for the cavas produced at the ultra-modern winery in Penedès are always sound and reliable and often excellent at the higher end of the range – notably the Chardonnay-influenced vintage Brut Nature and the splendid barrel-fermented Cuvée DS.

Gramona
08770 San Sadurní de Noya ☆☆☆☆
This much-admired, medium-sized family firm received many awards in 1997 for producing the best cavas.

The wines are handmade, with the same perfectionism as great Champagnes: hand-picked grapes; meticulous attention to blending details; and long ageing in bottle.

The standard Tira Extra Brut is genuinely dry and refreshingly crisp and clean. The Brut *rosé* has a lovely colour and bouquet, made from a successful blend of Monastrell, Grenache and Pinot Noir. The Tres Lustros Nature (70 per cent Xarel-lo) has five years on lees and superb depth of flavour. The Celler Battle is a stunning wine of remarkable complexity with a long maturation of over six years.

Huguet
08785 Cabrera de Noya ☆☆☆
This is a small family business with well-sited vineyards in the Alt Penedès, making an excellent Brut and a long-aged

Gran Reserva. They are progressive viticuturalists and are planting more Chardonnay and Pinot Noir. A name to watch.

J Freixedas Bove
08720 Vilafranca del Penedes ☆☆

A large *bodegas* founded at the turn of the century with a reputation for good cavas, and the Santa Mata range of Penedès table wines. Most grapes are bought in.

Juve y Camps
08770 San Sadurní de Noya ☆☆☆

Established in the 1920s, this firm makes superior dry cavas. In total, 60 per cent of the grapes come from the firm's own 400 hectares of vineyards, the remainder are bought in from selected growers under contract.

The top-flight Reserva de la Familia and Grand Cru are the favourite sparklers of the Spanish royal family and are stocked by the best restaurants and specialist wine shops.

Loxarel
08735 Vilobi del Penedès ☆☆

Good consistent quality from a firm that only makes cava from its own grapes.

From a wide range of sparkling wines, the Reserva Brut Nature and Reserva Familiar are especially recommended.

Marques de Monistrol
08770 Monistrol de Noya ☆☆

Now owned by Martini & Rossi, this *bodega* dominates the little white-washed village of Monistrol, where it has a large vineyard of 800 hectares.

About three quarters of production is cava, with a range of up to ten *cuvées*. The quality is quite sound, though the basic Brut is probably a better buy than the more expensive wines such as the Gran Tradición. The still Blanc en Noir and dry *rosé* are excellent wines.

Mascaro
08720 Vilafranca del Penedès ☆☆

This fine little family firm makes excellent Parellada-led cavas of refinement and vigour, way above the average.

Mascaro has also already planted Chardonnay at its two estates and a barrel-aged Cabernet Sauvignon is planned for the future.

Antonio Mestres Sagues
08770 San Sadurní de Noya ☆☆☆

A venerable gem of a *bodega*, dating back to 1312, this house makes exemplary cavas. Fragrant and of rare finesse, they are made entirely from the firm's own grapes, grown in a

90-hectare vineyard. The top-of-the-range Clos Nostre Senyor spends five years on lees before disgorging. The Los Cupages de Mestres range of cavas is younger, but beautifully made, and much in demand by Spain's best restaurants.

Mont Marcal
08732 Castellvi de la Marca ☆☆to☆☆☆

A progressive, quality-conscious family company which is making increasingly impressive cava in a fresh, aromatic, and pure-flavoured style.

These sparklers are very popular in the UK and the USA, with an excellent standard Brut and a fine Chardonnay-influenced Gran Reserva.

Bodegas Muga
26200 Haro ☆☆

This greatly admired *bodega* is best known for its superb Riojas, made by rigorously traditional methods.

The firm also makes a Viura-based sparkling wine in Brut and Brut-Nature *cuvées*, of good quality.

Ramón Nadal Giró
08733 El Pla del Penedès ☆☆

A specialist in vintage cavas, Ramón Nadal Giró makes a very good Brut Especial – structured and long flavoured – in outstanding years.

Albert i Noya
08738 San Pau d'Ordal ☆☆

A meticulously tended vineyard of Xarel-lo and Parellada grapes provides good raw material for the base wines of these very respectable cavas – a noteworthy *rosé* and Brut Nature. Fine aromatic still whites are also produced.

Cavas Rovellats
08731 San Marti de Sarroca ☆☆

A large cava producer with a 210-hectare estate. The Grand Extra Brut now has a refining touch of Chardonnay. Generally sound quality.

Heredia Segura Viudas
08770 Sant Sadurní de Noya ☆☆☆to☆☆☆☆

This is the model operation of the Freixenet empire, regularly producing sparkling wines with one of the best ratios of quality to price in the world.

The wines of associate company Conde de Caralt (qv) are made here, but the best grapes go into Segura Viudas' own blends. Everything in this cellar is well made and the best cavas, such as the Reserva Heredad and the vintage-dated Brut, can be superb.

The New World and other sparkling wine regions of the world

Sparkling wines are produced in 30 countries around the world. Almost invariably the best wines come from cool climate districts with enough acidity in their grapes to maintain the structure of a fine sparkler.

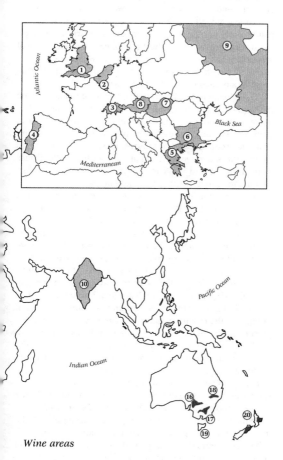

Wine areas

1. England
2. Luxembourg
3. Switzerland
4. Portugal
5. Greece
6. Bulgaria
7. Hungary
8. Austria
9. Russias
10. India
11. Canada
12. USA
13. Chile
14. Argentina
15. South Africa
16. South Australia
17. Victoria
18. New South Wales
19. Tasmania
20. New Zealand

California

Since the end of the Second World War, the expansion of the sparkling wine industry in California has been dramatic. As a result of phenomenal investment and modern technology, allied with a revival of the best traditional methods, the total production has risen to about 144 million bottles a year in the late 1990s. The domestic market is enormous, reflecting America's prodigious thirst for fizzy wine.

The leviathan of today started as a cottage industry in the mid-19th-century. Benjamin Davis Wilson was the first to make a Champagne-method sparkling wine in California in 1855. But, he and other early winemakers like the Sainsevain brothers, soon became discouraged by their inability to control the second sugar fermentation in bottle. Breakages were frequent and the wines undistinguished, their foxy flavours imparted by the native Mission grape.

A more determined effort to meet the challenge of the bubbles was made in 1867 by Arpad Haraszyth who, with the approval of his partners, pulled up his Mission vines and began to experiment with other grape varieties such as Riesling, Muscatel and Zinfandel. His best *cuvée*, Dry Eclipse, became a big success, symbolising the prosperity of the New Frontier. "Champagne is mother's milk to all these people," wrote Samuel Bowles, "they start the day with a Champagne cocktail and go to bed with a full bottle of it under their ribs."

The last quarter of the 19th century saw the founding of important firms whose sparkling wines are still strongly present in the market today – Almaden in 1876, Korbel in 1883 and Paul Masson in 1884. Each tried to perfect the *méthode champenoise* in California. The advent of Prohibition in 1919 brought sparkling winemaking in the USA to a virtual standstill. When the law was repealed in 1933, Almaden, Korbel and Paul Masson quickly went back into full-time business, though Haraszyth's Dry Eclipse disappeared.

With new producers appearing on the scene after 1933, the sparkling wine production technique known as the bulk (Charmat) method was employed increasingly. Sugar and yeasts were (and are) added in carefully measured amounts to the base wine. The second fermentation takes place in tank rather than bottle, and the resulting sparkling wine is then filtered before bottling. The result is a perfectly clean wine but one which lacks complexity or aptitude for ageing.

In the post-1945 period, the most successful technical development was the refining of the transfer method (qv), which seeks to combine the quality-first approach of bottle fermentation with more efficient and time-saving methods of processing. Sparkling wines made by the transfer method can be aged on lees for a longer period than is practicable in the bulk method, and the bubbles are more refined and long lived. By the early 1960s Almaden, Paul Masson and Weibel had all changed from the *méthode champenoise* to the transfer method. A revival of the classical hand-made approach to sparkling wine came in 1965, with the purchase of the defunct Schramsberg winery in Calistoga by Jack and Jamie Davies. The couple planted Pinot Noir, Chardonnay and Pinot Blanc and produced their wines with strict adherence to the Champagne method. Schramsberg's well-aged *cuvées* soon became the model for California's sparkling wines, by which all others were then judged, despite the increasingly stiff competition from new European ventures in California.

In the boom times of the '70s and '80s, the Champagne and cava houses of France and Spain, conscious of the vigour of the American market, invaded the Golden State, buying vineyards and setting up their own California sparkling wine subsidiaries. By the early '90s, the foreign presence in the vineyards of Napa and Sonoma read like a list of occupying powers – Moët & Chandon, at Domaine Chandon; Mumm, at Domaine Mumm; Roederer, at Domaine Roederer; Piper-Heidsieck, at Piper-Sonoma; Deutz, at Maison Deutz; Taittinger, at Domaine Carneros; Freixenet, at Gloria Ferrer; and Codorníu, at Codorníu Napa.

The ideal sites for growing sparkling wine grapes are still the subject of continuing research. Faced with the challenge of their hot climate, Californian vintners look for cooler sites where the grapes retain a decent level of acidity. Carneros, the district that straddles Napa and Sonoma, is a highly regarded source of well-balanced Pinot Noir and Chardonnay.

Domaine Chandon is increasingly attracted by the lively Chardonnays from the high-altitude vineyards of Mount Vedeer. And in the cool Green Valley of Sonoma, close to the ocean, Iron Horse is making impressive sparkling wines with a steely verve akin to Champagne. In the Anderson, Redwood, and Potter Valleys of Mendocino, fine California sparkling wine may find its most natural home – the superb current *cuvées* from Domaine Roederer and Handley, made here at the end of the 20th century, show how far the product has come in 150 years.

Tips for reading a California/USA sparkling wine label:
A sparkling wine made in California or any of the other 19 states of the Union may be called "Champagne". It is the one country in the world where this is still the case – the Champenois are attempting to suppress this usage in the courts, but so far (1998) without success.

Sparkling wines from the USA, made by the champagne or traditional method, do not have to specify their method of production on the label, but in practice often do. However, all bulk-method sparkling wines from the USA must specify their production method with words like "Charmat method", "transfer method", or any phrase which makes it clear that the wine was not fermented in the bottle. Terms like crackling or *frizzante* indicate a USA sparkling wine which bubbles less vigorously than Champagne.

The relative levels of dryness to sweetness are signalled by such words as Naturel or Brut Zero; Brut; Sec; and Demi-sec – following the Champagne tradition. However, the amount of sugar in any Brut blend can vary widely from brand to brand throughout the USA.

Adler Fells
Santa Rosa Ca 95409 ☆

Founded in 1980 by David Coleman, this is a small Sonoma winery overlooking the Valley of the Moon on a ledge called Eagle Rock (or Adler Fels in German).

Admired for its rich, full Chardonnay and clean, well-made Fumé Blanc; a tiny amount of traditional-method sparkling wine is also produced from a blend of Riesling and Gewürztraminer.

Almaden Vineyards
San Joaquin Ca 91320 ☆

One of the earliest firms making sparkling wine in California (1876). Almaden now produces about six million bottles a year of sound, clean, transfer-method bubbly under such labels as Golden Champagne and Eye of the Partridge. A big market across the USA.

Andre (E & J Gallo)
Modesto Ca 95353 ☆

The best-selling bulk-method California sparkler from the world's biggest wine company; available in Brut, Extra Dry and pink versions. Quality is sound; the wines clean tasting. Production of around 12 million bottles a year.

Château St Jean
Kenwood Ca 95452 ☆☆☆

This winery was bought from Suntory by Beringer in 1996. Château St Jean is consolidating its fine reputation for opulent Chardonnays and sweet, *botrytis* Rieslings and Traminers, while increasing production of red varietal wines, notably Cabernet Sauvignon.

The estate still makes the excellent vintage-dated Grand Cuvée sparkling wine, with at least six years on lees. The 1989 was released on the market in March 1998.

The Christian Brothers
Rutherford Ca 94573 ☆

This Catholic order of lay brothers from Champagne used to make still and sparkling wines in the Napa Valley. Now the label is used exclusively as a brandy-only label for Heublein. Old stocks of Brother Timothy's birthday bubbly are still good, if you can manage to find a bottle.

Codorníu Napa
Napa Ca 94558 ☆☆
This is the Californian outpost of the Codorníu Spanish cava empire, and is on track to produce around eight million bottles a year of traditional-method sparkling wine by the end of the 20th century.

All the Pinot Noir and Chardonnay grapes for the blends come from the company's 100 hectares of vineyards – the best are situated in the cooler Carneros. Also, excellent Carneros-derived Blanc de Noirs.

Domaine Carneros
Carneros Ca ☆☆☆
Founded in 1987 with Taittinger Champagne as the major shareholder, this is one of the best French-owned sparkling wine enterprises – using only top-quality grapes, exclusively from Carneros.

Both the 1991 Brut and the 1990 Blanc de Blancs are impressively structured yet silky wines. The still Carneros red wine is also excellent. The winery itself has been designed in a *grandiose* French style.

Domaine Chandon
Yountville Ca 94599 ☆☆☆*to*☆☆☆☆
The first French-owned Californian producer of sparkling wine. Founded in 1973, with a proven track record in providing both quantity and quality at realistic prices.

The Reserve bottlings of Pinot Noir, with four years on lees, are excellent, rich and creamy. The new Carneros-sourced Blanc de Blancs is a winner, and the super Reserve Etoile is top flight. The exciting quality here owes everything to Dawneen Dwyer, one of the most open-minded and informative of winemakers. Its own restaurant, under chef Philippe Jeanty (a Champenois), is one of the best in the USA.

Geyser Peak Winery
Geyserville CA 95441 ☆
An old winery, bought by Henry Trion in the 1980s. It offers a wide range of wines made by Australian Daryl Groom.

Good traditional-method Brut, made from Alexander Valley and Russian River fruit.

Glen Ellen Winery (Benzinger)
Glen Ellen CA 95442 ☆☆
The Benzinger family sold its Glen Ellen brands to the Heublein group, and now concentrates full-time on its

Imagery series of limited-release wines. These include a vintage-dated Blanc de Blancs sparkler which is partly vinified in wood.

Gloria Ferrer
Sonoma CA 95476 ☆☆

This winery was established in 1986 close to Los Pablos Bay in the Sonoma region.

Gloria Ferrer is named after the wife of the President of Freixenet, the giant Spanish cava producer which owns this winery. They make good classically made sparkling wines which are produced in volume. Especially noteworthy are the Blanc de Noirs and excellent Cuvée Carneros.

The winery is an easy drive north of San Francisco (*see* also Freixenet, Spain and Henri Abelé, Champagne).

Handley Cellars
Philo CA 95446 ☆☆☆☆

An outstanding producer of sparkling wines, handmade from first-class grapes in the cool Anderson Valley.

This small family firm is almost self-sufficient in grapes, producing around 18,000 bottles a year from a five-hectare vineyard. Superb Brut rosé and Blanc de Blancs.

Iron Horse Vineyards
Sebastopol CA 95472 ☆☆☆☆

An excellent sparkling wine producer, with superb hilltop vineyards, above the cool Green Valley, and close to the ocean. Owner Forrest Tancer is a Pinot Noir devotee and probably knows more about where to grow it successfully in California than anybody else.

His expertise shows in the Blanc de Noirs Wedding Cuvée – aromatic and ample, deliciously fruity, yet surprisingly complex. A great wine, as is his fine-drawn, still Pinot Noir, which I was lucky enough to enjoy at Forrest Tancer's hospitable table in 1994.

Iron Horse is involved in a joint venture here with the de Nonancourt family of Laurent-Perrier Champagne (qv).

Jordan Vineyards
Healdsburg CA 95448 ☆☆to☆☆☆☆

Since the 1990 vintage, the "J" luxury sparkling *cuvée* from Jordan has improved markedly, now steering a good middle course between ripe California fruit character and the looked-for austere tautness of Champagne.

The grape mix is a blend of 50 per cent each of Pinot Noir and Chardonnay, mainly sourced from the Russian River area and the Jordan's own 44-hectare Ranch vineyard.

They also produce a superb, cedary Cabernet Sauvignon which is a delight.

Korbel
Guerneville CA 95446 ☆

Founded in 1883, Korbel remains a big-time producer of soft, traditional and transfer-method sparkling wines geared to the American palate. And clearly its loyal clientele like the range – drinking 12 million bottles a year.

Two new releases: sprightly Korbel Chardonnay (75 per cent) Champagne; and for collectors, richly flavoured Limited Edition Frank Sinatra Cuvée, a fitting salute to ol' blue eyes.

Thomas Kruse Winery
Gilroy CA 95020 ☆☆

In the Santa Cruz mountains, south of San Francisco Bay, Kruse makes minuscule quantities of bone-dry *méthode-traditionelle* wine with minimal *dosage*.

Pinot Noir dominates the blend and Insouciance is its main label.

Maison Deutz
Arroya Grande CA 93420 ☆☆

A Franco-American joint venture of the early 1980s, with the much-respected Champagne Deutz of Aÿ providing the sparkling expertise. The San Luis Obispo location provides a coolish site close to the ocean.

The wines have a reputation for being rich and old-fashioned, and are dominated by Pinot Noir. However, following its takeover by Roederer, Deutz is no longer involved in the venture.

Paul Masson Vineyards
Saratoga 95070 CA ☆☆

The giant Paul Masson company – one of the earliest in the sparkling wine field – continues to make some of the better transfer-method wines in both Brut and Extra Dry versions. They have a freshness unmatched by the competition.

Mirassou Champagne Cellars
Los Gatos CA 95032 ☆☆☆

A respected, long-established firm founded by a French-born gold prospector in the 1850s. The Pinot Noir, Chardonnay, and Pinot Blanc grapes come from the firm's well-sited vineyards in Monterey, where the ocean-affected climate is clement. Excellent well-aged Brut Reserve, produced with strict adherence to classical methods.

Robert Mondavi
Oakville CA 94562 ☆☆☆

Robert Mondavi is America's best-known vintner, and his son Tim is an endlessly curious winemaker. They constantly experiment with Champagne-method sparkling wines and offer occasional limited releases of admirably made *cuvées*, often part-fermented in wood, and always with at least four years on lees. The wines are only for sale at the winery, but it is certainly worth the effort to try them.

Domaine Mumm
Silverado Trail, Napa CA 94558 ☆☆☆

The Seagram-owned *grande marque* Mumm Champagne opened its glittering California winery in 1983, and it has consistently outshone its Reims parent since the first vintage in 1986. The whole range shares a vibrant, pure-fruit style that is very Californian.

The pick of the bunch are the outstanding Brut Prestige (a real ☆☆☆☆ wine); the yeasty-rich Vintage Reserve (lovely 1987); and the exuberant Blanc de Noirs. Most *cuvées* prefer a grape mix of 60 per cent Pinot Noir, 40 per cent Chardonnay.

Parsons Creek Winery
Ukiah CA 95482 ☆☆☆

This boutique winery in Mendocino County was making potentially excellent traditional-method sparkling wines from Potter and Anderson Valley Pinot Noir and Chardonnay grapes in the early 1990s.

Unfortunately we have been unable to establish contact here recently. Readers' comments welcome.

Piper Sonoma
Healdsburg CA 95448 ☆☆

Established in 1980, another Franco-American joint venture, with Piper-Heidsieck of Reims providing the Champagne-method expertise.

The wine style has been lean and tight knit in the Piper mould from the start. Correct winemaking, with occasionally excellent *cuvées* such as the vintage-dated Tête de Cuvée.

Martin Ray Vineyards
Palo Alto CA 94303 ☆☆☆

This winery was the first to plant Pinot Noir and Chardonnay for Champagne-method sparkling wines in the early 1960s.

With high-quality grapes, from cool Santa Cruz Mountain vineyards, it makes excellent Naturel Cuvée (minimal *dosage*).

Roederer Estate
Philo CA 95466 ☆☆☆☆

This is Champagne-house Louis Roederer's 1980s California venture and it has been a triumph, for the chosen 140-hectare vineyard site in the cool Anderson Valley is a perfect one.

The 1989 L'Ermitage top *cuvée* is a stunning success, and as close in style and complexity to the real thing as it is possible to be.

Scharffenberger Cellars
Philo CA 95466 ☆☆☆

These are ambitious Mendocino County traditional-method winemakers with 60 hectares of excellent Pinot Noir and Chardonnay, mostly in the Anderson Valley. Their serious, unhurried procedures include ageing all the *cuvées* for at least three years on lees.

The flagship Brut is admirably clean and citrussy, with an attractive end note of mature autolytic flavours. Champagne Pommery owns shares in the company.

Schramsberg Vineyards
Calistoga CA94515 ☆☆☆☆

This historic winery was established on the hillsides of Calistoga by Jacob Schram in 1862 and was known to the British writer Robert Louis Stevenson.

It was bought and restored by Jack and Jamie Davies in 1965, and Schramsberg was the first to make traditional-method sparkling wines from the classic Champagne grapes. The wines are still among the most complex around – a long lees ageing; use of reserve wine (which is uncommon in California); and rigorous blending are the keys to quality. Excellent Blanc de Noirs; superb Brut Reserve; and the very classy, part-wood-fermented J Schram, made from primarily Chardonnay grapes

The much-loved Jack Davies died in 1998.

Shadow Creek
Yountville CA 94599 ☆☆to☆☆☆

Now owned by Domaine Chandon and also being produced at Yountville, this is a selection of sparkling wines which provides terrific value for money.

On the whole, this label offers a highly respectable range of dry styles – from the Brut to the Blanc de Blancs – and at very reasonable prices.

Weibel Vineyards
San Jose CA94539 ☆

Founded by the Swiss Weibel family, the future of this Mendocino County winery is now uncertain, but it is still producing wine. The mainly tank-method sparklers are made in a soft uncomplicated style; the old champagne-method premium *cuvée* was always a good wine.

Wente Bros
Livermore CA 94550 ☆

A very long-established family wine firm with a modern sparkling wine *cuverie,* which was renovated in 1981.

Three good sparklers culminating in the Chardonnay-led Grande Reserve, from good Monterey grapes.

Rest of USA

Nicholas Longworth made the first sparkling wine in the United States, in the state of Ohio in 1842. He called the wine "Sparkling Catawba" after the native Catawba grape he used to produce it.

Today sparkling wine is made in at least 20 states of the Union, but most of it comes from two – California and New York. In many other states, with the exception of those in the clement Pacific NorthWest, the harshness of the winters and the lateness of the springs restrict the choice of viable grape varieties to hardy American and French hybrids.

Most American hybrids, especially the Concord, have a strong "foxy" flavour – generally alien to international wine tastes; but French hybrids, such as Seyval Blanc and Vidal, give much better results. In regions where the American winter is not impossibly severe, the best sparklers are increasingly those made by the Champagne method, using "traditional" grapes.

ARKANSAS
Post Familie Vineyards
Altus AR 72821 ☆☆

At Altus, between Fort Smith and Little Rock, Andrew Post makes good traditional sparkling wine from both Chardonnay and hybrid grape varieties.

CONNECTICUT
Haight Vineyard
Litchfield CT 06759 ☆☆

Sherman Haight converted a hay barn into a winery in 1978 and five years later made the first Connecticut "Champagne". The quality of the Blanc de Blancs, mainly Seyval Blanc with a little Chardonnay, is very sound.

IDAHO
Sainte Chapelle Winery
Caldwell ID 83605 ☆☆

Winemaker Kevin Mott is consolidating the reputation of this, the largest of Idaho's wineries.

The racy, floral sparkling wines sensibly rely on a high proportion of Riesling – a grape that suits Idaho's chilly climate. Pinot Noir and Chardonnay are also grown on the 460-acre estate to source the superior Brut Reserve.

ILLINOIS
Thompson Winery
Monee IL 60449 ☆

A 30-acre Illinois winery, housed in a converted railway station, and celebrated for its bottle-fermented "Champagne" made from French hybrid and *labrusca* grapes.

MAINE
Bartlett Maine Estate Winery
Gouldsboro ME 04607 ☆

This cellar is equipped for serious winemaking – from the French oak barrels to the riddling *pupitres*.

However, the raw material is not grapes, but apples and pears, which they make into a sparkling fruit wine, aged on lees for five years. Worth a try.

MASSACHUSETTS
Chicama Vineyards
West Tisbury MA 02575 ☆

This winery was established on Martha'a Vineyard in 1971. George and Catherine Mathiesen are admired for their good Sea Mist sparkling wine made from *vinifera* grape varieties.

MICHIGAN
Fenn Valley Vineyards
Fennville MI 49408 ☆☆

Owner Doug Welsch is the best winemaker in Michigan. He is a pacesetter in planting European varietals, and produces a fine sparkling Blanc de Blancs from pure Riesling.

Leelanau Wine Cellars
Omena MI 49674 ☆

Northern Michigan's largest winery with a spectacular view of Grand Traverse Bay. They produce a good barrel-fermented Chardonnay and increasingly respectable sparkling wine from the Champagne grapes.

Tabor Hill
Buchanan MI 49107 ☆

A Michigan winery (and restaurant) favoured by Gerald Ford when he was President. Tabor Hill produces a creditable "Grand Mark" sparkler from Pinot Noir and Chardonnay; also a sweetish Italian-style *spumante*. Sound quality.

MISSOURI
Hermannhof
Hermannhof MO 65041 ☆to☆☆

A national historic site since 1852, sporting one of the largest wine halls in America. Hermannhof makes sparklers mainly from French hybrids. Also, good Seyval-based Blanc de Blancs.

Rosati Winery
St James MO 65559 ☆

This winery takes its name from the Rosati area around St James, where Italian immigrants became fruit growers and winemakers in the 1890s. Its easy-drinking sparklers are made from *labrusca* grapes.

St James Winery
St James MO 65559 ☆

This is an award-winning winery, and was founded in 1973 by the Hoffherr family. They produce everything from fruit juice and mead, to wine and "Champagne".

The younger Hoffherrs went to wine school in California and are now making their bottle-fermented sparklers from the Champagne grape varieties.

NEW JERSEY
Renault Winery
Egg Harbor City NJ 08215 ☆

This estate was established in 1864 by Louis N Renault, the agent for Montebello Champagne. This East Coast winery produces around 273,000 litres (60,000 gallons) of wine a year, in a myriad of styles.

Their sparklers range from "blueberry Champagne" to a much improved bottle-fermented "white Champagne" – made from French hybrid and classic varieties.

NEW YORK STATE

New York is an important source of wine. It has 12,000 hectares under vine – roughly equivalent to that of the Alsace winefield in France. Historically, the Finger Lakes district, in the central part of the state, has been home for over a century to a considerable sparkling wine industry, based on American and French hybrid grape varieties such as Catawba, Delaware and Seyval Blanc.

In the west, along the shores of Lake Erie and extending through New York, Pennsylvania and Ohio, is a sizeable vineyard area, of which a part is devoted to sparkling wine grapes. In downstate New York towards Manhattan, the Hudson Valley has an old vine-growing tradition, established by early colonists in the 1690s and now rejuvenated by the emergence of some promising new wineries such as Milbrook Vineyards.

In recent years, winemakers have come to realise that New York's cold marginal climate is much closer to that of Champagne than California's, and that it could provide a more favourable environment in which classic sparkling wine grapes might flourish. Back in the 1950s, Charles Fournier, ex-Veuve Clicquot and the head winemaker at the Gold Seal winery in the Finger Lakes, initiated experimental plantings of Chardonnay, Riesling and Pinot Blanc for the purposes of sparkling wine production.

Now, 40 years on – and thanks to superior clones and vinification techniques – good classic sparkling wines are being made, especially by Great Western, Glenora and McGregor. Not that there is anything intrinsically wrong with the hybrid sparklers. Clinton vineyards, in the Hudson

Valley, makes an excellent "Champagne" entirely from Seyval Blanc grapes. By 1996, New York had 101 wineries, of which 77 had been established in the previous 20 years. Around one-fifth of these produce sparkling wines of a standard that deserve wider attention from sparkler lovers outside America.

Barrington Champagne Company
Dundee NY 14837 ☆☆
Chardonnay grapes from the Finger Lakes dominate and define the blend of the Barrington Blanc de Blancs.

All the Champagne-method processes, including hand riddling, are strictly adhered to here.

Casa Larga Vineyards
Fairport NY 14838 ☆☆
There are 6,000 bottles of the pure Chardonnay Casa Larga Naturel (minimal *dosage*), made every year from the estate's Finger Lakes grapes – brisk, incisive, and a very good *apéritif.*

Clinton Vineyards
Clinton Corners NY 12514 ☆☆☆
Who says all great bubbly is made from Pinot Noir and Chardonnay? This Champagne-method 100-per-cent Seyval Blanc has all the vinous Chablis-like character of this very underrated hybrid. Great flavour for little outlay.

The winery is just a short drive north of Manhattan, in the Hudson River Valley.

De May Wine Cellars
Hammondsport NY 14840 ☆
A French family from the Loire Valley established this small boutique winery in the Finger Lakes. Well-made bottle-fermented sparklers in all styles – dry, medium and sweet – are available only directly from the winery.

Domaine Charbaut
Seneka Lake NY 14839 ☆☆
Charbaut was one of the first Epernay Champagne houses to see the potential of New York State for sparkling wine, acquiring an option on upstate land in 1990.

To date, the grapes – mainly Chardonnay – are bought in from the Finger Lakes region, but the policy is eventually to grow all the grapes on their own estate. Serious and careful winemaking *a la façon* Champenoise.

Glenora Wine Cellars
Dundee NY 14837 ☆☆☆
Every aspect of this boutique, quality-first operation inspires confidence. Controlled sales (100,000 bottles a year) of

hand-crafted, properly aged *cuvées,* based mainly on the estate's own Pinot Noir, Pinot Blanc and Chardonnay grapes.

They produce an excellent Blanc de Blancs Naturel, and a fine ageworthy Brut Reserve.

Gold Seal Vineyards
Hammondsport NY 14840 ☆to☆☆

This is one of the first wineries in the Finger Lakes region – founded in 1865. The historic firm has a long association with Champenois winemakers.

The best known of them, Charles Fournier, began his work in the 1950s with classic *vinifera* grape varieties such as Chardonnay and Pinot Blanc for his *méthode champenoise* wines. The top-of-the-range Charles Fournier *cuvées* are still made this way.

However there are also a plethora of cheaper blends made by the transfer method from a hotchpotch of *labrusca* and hybrid varieties. The firm is now owned by The Taylor Wine Company, in turn part of Seagram.

Great Western
Hammondsport NY 14840 ☆to☆☆☆

Founded in 1860 and now part of the Seagram stable, this is the oldest sparkling wine firm in the Finger Lakes region.

The range of wines, and quality, is wide – from the transfer-method Cold Duck and hugely successful Great Western Natural New York "Champagne" to the Champagne-method Blanc de Blancs, a true ☆☆☆ wine, probably rivaling California's finest sparklers.

Knapp Vineyards
Romulus NY 14541 ☆to☆☆

In 1971 Doug and Suzie Knapp converted a 100-acre chicken farm into a vineyard.

They now produce an admired *méthode-champenoise* Chardonnay-led Brut, and also have their own restaurant.

McGregor Vineyard
Dundee NY 14837 ☆☆☆

The McGregors planted this excellent 28-acre estate with classic grape varieties in 1980.

They produce a first-rate *méthode-champenoise* Blanc de Blanc (a pure Chardonnay), a Blanc de Noirs, as well as a sparkling Riesling.

Millbrook Vineyards
Milbrook NY 12545 ☆☆☆

One of the Hudson Valley's newest wineries, already making some finely wrought Champagne-method sparklers – the best is based on Chardonnay.

Schapiro's Wine Company
New York NY 10002 ☆

Norman Schapiro directs this thriving Kosher winery, established by his grandfather Sam in the 1890s. Beth Din approved wines, from Heavy Concord to Cold Duck and Sparkling Burgundy.

The Taylor Wine Company
Hammondsport NY 14840 ☆

Founded in 1880, Taylor is the giant of the three Seagram-owned wineries in the Finger Lakes region (*see also* Gold Seal and Great Western).

Huge volumes of sparkling wines are made here by the transfer method, and this has earned the company the nickname of, "the Coca Cola of the wine business".

However, the French and American hybrid-based wines are soundly made.

Hermann J Wiemer
Dundee NY 14837 ☆☆

Hermann Wiemer was trained at Geisenheim and quickly established a reputation as one of the best winemakers in New York State. The Riesling grape is the source of the very good bottle-fermented Brut.

Woodbury Vineyards
Dunkirk NY 14048 ☆☆

This estate has been the leading grape grower of New York State's Chautauqua county since 1910. The Woodbury family built a new winery in 1979, specialising in Chardonnay, the source of their excellent bottle-fermented Blanc de Blancs.

NORTH CAROLINA
Biltmore Estate Wine Company
Asheville NC28803 ☆☆

Built at the turn of the century by the fabulously wealthy George Vanderbilt, the Biltmore mansion and estate is a glittering showpiece of the south.

The Pinot Noir and Chardonnay vines, planted by their French winemaker in the mid-1980s, are now approaching maturity and provide the base for very good Champagne method sparkling wines. Château Biltmore, sourced entirely from the Vanderbilts' own grapes, is the best *cuvée*.

OHIO
Mantey Vineyards
Sanduskey OH 44870 ☆

A late 19th-century winery, overlooking Lake Erie, now equipped with modern means to make Charmat-method sparklers from mainly Seyval Blanc.

Stillwaters Winery
West Troy OH 45373 ☆

This winery takes its name from the Stillwaters river and, paradoxically, specialises in the production of sparkling wine.

Classic bottle-fermentation of Seyval and Vidal wines gives a good result in their respected Brut.

OREGON

Situated between California and Washington State, Oregon has a temperate climate. Close to the Pacific ocean, its vineyards are directly exposed to marine breezes, resulting in mild winters and long cool summers. This is ideal territory in which to grow Pinot Noir and Chardonnay for the production of sparkling wine, as the grapes have fine clarity of flavour due to lower alcohol and higher acidity.

The winemakers of Oregon are a quiet group of stubborn individualists, more absorbed in the intricacies of their craft than in the black arts of marketing and self promotion. But since the arrival of the internationally known Australian-wine-*supremo* Brian Croser at Argyle in 1987, Oregon has gained press plaudits for its potential to produce world class sparkling wine – already fine enough to give the Champenois pause for thought.

These are early days for this particular state of the USA; for there are merely a handful of recommended producers, but the future certainly looks bright, as foreign investors come to realise the full potential of Oregan as a producer of sparkling wines.

Argyle
Dundee OR 97115 ☆☆☆☆

This is a joint venture, launched in 1987 by Brian Croser of Petaluma, Australia and C Calvert Knudsden, the founder of the Erath Vineyard and Winery in Oregon's Williamette Valley (qv).

Most of the classic Pinot Noir and Chardonnay grapes for the traditional-method *cuvées* come from immaculately tended, low-yielding vines in the Dundee Hills.

Extended ageing on lees (up to five years) has contributed to an exceptionally fine, vintage-dated Brut, which is a blend of 60 per cent Pinot Noir and 40 per cent Chardonnay (the 1988, 1990 and 1992 are all top flight). Very stylish Blanc de Blancs, and a lovely pure Pinot Noir *rosé*.

Arterberry
McMinnville OR 97128 ☆☆

The first Champagne-method Oregon sparklers were made under this label, at Oregon pioneer David Letts' Eyrie vineyard in the Williamette Valley.

The wines are vintage dated, and the *dosage* is low.

Château Benoit
Carlton OR 97111 ☆☆

An enlarged 75-acre estate in the Williamette Valley run with care and commitment by the Benoit family. The Brut, a classic mix of Pinot Noir and Chardonnay, is recommended.

Erath Vineyard and Winery
Dundee OR 97115 ☆☆

Formerly Knudsen Erath, this large Dundee Hills estate and winery has a new partner and winemaker, Rob Stuart.

The wines range from Pinot Gris to Arneis and Dolcetto, and are eclectic but good; plus they include a fine *méthode champenoise* Brut.

Laurel Ridge Winery
Forest Grove OR 97116 ☆☆

David and Susan Teppola are committed to making sparkling wine in commercially viable quantities. Their new eight-hectare Chardonnay and Pinot Noir vineyard has just come into production, supplementing their already established 22-hectare holdings in the Williamette Valley.

The quality is good too, from the Riesling-based Cuvée Blanc to the Pinot-led Brut. Also a well-aged Brut Reserve.

St Innocent Winery
Salem OR 97302 ☆☆

A new Oregon winery founded in 1988. So far producing two sparkling wines by the Champagne method.

A three-year-old Brut (60 per cent Pinot Noir and 40 per cent Chardonnay) and a six-year-old Reserve Cuvée. The winemaker is originally from Arterberry (qv).

PENNSYLVANIA
Penn Shore Vineyards
North East PA 16428 ☆

Founded in 1968, and located on the southern shores of Lake Erie. Vidal and other French hybrids source their sparklers.

TEXAS
La Buena Vida Vineyards
Springtown TX 76082 ☆

The Smith family grow mainly hybrid grapes in their vineyard just outside Fort Worth. They make well-balanced traditional-method sparkling wines.

VIRGINIA
Ingleside Plantation Vineyards
Oak Grove VA 22443 ☆☆

This Médocain winemaker produces a very good (still) Cabernet Sauvignon, and a fine *méthode-champenoise* wine based on Pinot Noir and Chardonnay. The latter is definitely an advance on the first hybrid-based sparklers made here.

Oasis Vineyard
Hume VA 22639 ☆☆

An easy drive from Washington DC *en route* to the Blue Mountains. This is a sizeable vineyard and is planted with Chardonnay and Pinot Noir, from which are produced some very well-made sparklers by both the transfer and traditional methods. Royal Pink Cuvée is particularly recommended.

Rapidan River Vineyards
Culpeper VA 22725 ☆

With German-style grapes and winemaking, this is the style to expect here. There is a clean pure-flavoured sparkling Riesling, which is recommended. The facility is owned by the Prince Michel winery.

WASHINGTON STATE
Château Ste-Michelle
Woodinville WA 99350 ☆☆☆

By far the biggest winery in the Pacific Northwest, the vineyard was planted in the 1950s.

Mike Januit leads a team of proficient winemakers who produce a broad range of classic red and white varietals. The traditional-method sparkling wines are elegant and aromatic, notably the pure-flavoured Blanc de Blancs and the mature Blanc de Noirs – aged on lees for five years. Quality has surged ahead in the '90s.

Mountain Dome Winery
Spokane WA 99207 ☆☆☆

In the lee of Mount Spokane, the Manzs are perfectionists and are focused entirely on making the best possible sparkling wines they can.

They harvest the Pinot Noir, Chardonnay and Pinot Meunier grapes in the Columbia River Valley by hand; ferment the base wines in wood; use only the *méthode champenoise*; and after the *prise de mousse,* the wines are aged on lees for 48 months.

The classically assembled Brut; the expressive Pinot-led *rosé;* and the sumptuous Blanc de Noirs are all excellent. Forrest Tancer and his winemakers at the peerless Iron Horse in California (qv) are consultants here.

Preston Cellars
Pasco WA 99301 ☆☆

Bill Preston's son Brent is now the winemaker at this well-sited 170-acre vineyard close to the junction of the Columbia and Snake rivers. Good *méthode-champenoise* bubbly.

Australia

Australia's quality sparkling wine industry is of fairly recent provenance. The climate that prevails in most of its premium growing areas is scarcely comparable to that of Champagne. As a result, early attempts at fizz often had an overripe tropical flavour that Europeans found cloying. The advances in technology, and particularly more careful selection of vineyard sites in the 1980s, were responsible for transforming that picture. Modest amounts of imported expertise from Champagne houses such as Moët & Chandon and Louis Roederer have also played their part.

The pre-eminent state for sparkling wines has traditionally been Victoria, notably the Great Western and Drumborg regions, and other zones in the central sector of the state. Here is where most of the famous names in Australian fizz are located. Ballarat, about 75 miles northwest of Melbourne, is considered a particularly promising district. Cooler sites in neighbouring South Australia, such as the Adelaide Hills, are now being explored, and there is a dogged determination among a handful of producers to obtain classic sparklers from the very cool vineyards of Tasmania – so far with distinctly patchy results, it has to be said.

Most producers use the Champagne duo of Pinot Noir and Chardonnay in their wines (there are only tiny, but growing, enclaves of Pinot Meunier here), and use of the Champagne method is widespread. Cheaper everyday sparklers are likely to have been made by the transfer method.

The innovative and singular contribution of Australia to world sparkling wine production is the sparkling reds made from Cabernet Sauvignon or Shiraz – some are bone-dry and tannic, others sweeter and softer. These are finding increasing commercial favour.

All Saints
Rutherglen Victoria ☆☆
Acquired by the bulk-producers Brown Brothers in 1992, All Saints is not only a highly respected maker of fortified wines, but also produces a state-of-the-art sparkling red from Cabernet Sauvignon.

The wines are full of rich, ripe blackcurrant fruit, with a tinge of sweetness on the finish.

Ashton Hills
Adelaide Hills South Australia ☆☆
This winery was founded only in the 1990s by winemaker Stephen George, and takes advantage of the microclimate in one of South Australia's cooler areas to produce a classic, bottle-fermented Chardonnay and Pinot Noir sparkler called Salmon Brut. The style of the wine is delicate and fresh, with a crisp appley tang.

Barossa Valley Estates
Barossa Valley South Australia ☆☆

This is a constituent part of the BRL Hardy empire, making a range of sparklers in widely varying styles. Its flagship is probably the E & E Black Pepper Sparkling Shiraz, which is a monumentally dense, rich, purple wine with fairly heavyweight tannin, and appreciable quantities of the hot spice alluded to in the name.

A secondary range, Killawarra, includes a yeasty Vintage Brut, as well as an everyday *rosé*, which shows attractive light strawberry notes.

BRL Hardy
McLaren Vale South Australia ☆

The gigantic Hardy combine owns a number of well-known labels, as well as having interests in the south of France.

Its sparkling wines include a convincingly toasty Pinot Noir-Chardonnay NV, as well as the more recently released Nottage Hill Sparkling Chardonnay – a light-textured fizz, with more than a hint of tropical fruit on the palate.

Brown Brothers
Milawa Victoria ☆☆

This long-established family company numbers among its many *cuvées* a Pinot Noir-Chardonnay Brut sparkler made in Victoria's King Valley. Now fairly widely distributed, its style is lemon-fresh clean – distinct aromas of yeast autolysis on the nose and a strong, persistent finish.

Cofield
Rutherglen Victoria ☆☆

One of Victoria's newer wineries has made something of a name for itself locally as a boutique-scale producer of sparkling reds.

Its Shiraz is a mightily powerful, blackberry-fruited wine of rich, creamy texture, and good supporting acidity.

Cranswick Estate
Riverina New South Wales ☆

Winemaker Graham Smith is responsible for the Pinot Noir-Chardonnay Brut NV of this winery.

It is aged on lees for three years before being disgorged, but is nonetheless curiously light in body, with an odd but not unattractive floral perfume and flavour.

Deakin Estate
Mildura Victoria ☆☆

Part of the Wingara wine group, Deakin makes a rich, tropical-flavoured sparkler, Deakin Estate Brut, that supports its intense fruitiness with a high-octane 13.5 per cent alcohol.

De Bortoli Wines
Murrumbidgee Irrigation Area New South Wales ☆

Dessert wine specialists De Bortoli now own vineyards in Victoria, source of their Windy Peak Sparkling NV – discreet on the nose, but with exotic mango-like fruit on the palate.

Domaine Chandon
Yarra Valley Victoria ☆☆☆☆

Champagne giant Moët & Chandon has investments in three continents – including here in Australia. Commitment to quality has been enhanced by the winemaking skills of the charismatic Dr Tony Jordan – an uncompromising standard bearer for Australian fizz.

On the export markets, the wines are labelled Green Point, and the range takes in Vintage Brut of considerable finesse and lightly lemony vintage-dated Blanc de Blancs.

The vintage *rosé* (particularly the 1993) is full of fruity complexity. All are made by the traditional method.

Dromana Estate
Mornington Peninsula Victoria ☆

The secondary label of Dromana is called, Schinus Molle. The range includes a NV Chardonnay-Pinot Noir made in a fresh, clean, inoffensive style.

Garden Gulley
Great Western Victoria ☆☆

These are recognised sparkling wine specialists, headed by Brian Fletcher (ex-Seppelt).

The traditional method is used to make lush-textured wines, which are unashamedly sold in their native territory as "Sparkling Burgundy".

Hanging Rock
Macedon Victoria ☆☆

Based in a newly-developed vineyard area in central Victoria, Hanging Rock is an ambitious operation that has nailed its colours to the sparkling wine mast. The NV Brut is a complex, yeasty fizz, and fermented in the bottle.

Heemskerk
Launceston Tasmania ☆☆

This house was established in the sparkling stakes by Champagne house Louis Roederer in the 1980s (and then left to go it alone again in 1994), their vintage-dated sparkling wine is called Janz.

Although early attempts were less than persuasive – owing in part to sloppy vineyard management in this marginal climate – most of the vintages of the 1990s have been impressive for their steely, palate cleansing style.

Hollick Wines

Coonawarra South Australia ☆☆☆

Ian Hollick's winery, founded in 1983, is situated in an area more reputed for robust reds than sparklers.

However, the Cornel Vintage Brut – made from a blend of Pinot Noir and Chardonnay, with secondary fermentation in the bottle – is a pace-setting wine in terms of sheer exuberant class and length of flavour.

Charles Melton

Barossa Valley South Australia ☆☆☆

Charles Melton undoubtedly grows some of the most shatteringly concentrated Shiraz in the Barossa Valley, and uses a proportion of it to make an exemplary sparkling red.

The ultra-ripe and powerful fruit on the palate combines all the bramble-scented beauty of this grape with firm, underpinning tannins to produce a soundly structured sparkler. It is one of the benchmark wines currently being made in this style.

Moorilla Estate

Hobart Tasmania ☆

This is among the southernmost wineries on Tasmania, Moorilla – which has been producing wine here since the 1960s – capitalises on the prevailing cool climate conditions to make sparkling wines from Pinot Noir and Chardonnay by the traditional method.

The Vintage Brut encapsulates the style with crisp, lemony acidity and gentle yeastiness.

Orlando

Barossa Valley South Australia ☆

The French-owned Orlando group is unquestionably good at crowd-pleasing, commercial wines – typified by the best-selling Jacob's Creek range.

As one would expect, its sparkling wines are made in an approachable low-acid, generously dosed style. The Carrington Brut Rosé is a deservedly popular strawberry-fruited pink wine, with plenty of easy-going charm.

Petaluma

Adelaide Hills South Australia ☆☆☆

The highly talented Brian Croser includes among his *repertoire* a vintage-dated sparkler called, modestly enough, Croser. Vintages such as the '93 and '94 – both excellent – are marked by yeasty tones on the nose and sharp-edged, appley fruit on the palate. Both have a gentle creamy finish.

At its best, this winery could be one of the few serious rivals to Domaine Chandon's Green Point for the Australian sparkling wine crown.

Seaview Winery
McLaren Vale South Australia ☆☆☆

A component part of Australia's massive Southcorp wine organisation, Seaview has been a specialist producer of sparkling wine for many years.

Its range includes a simple NV Brut of no great distinction, a delicately textured Rosé Brut NV with hints of cranberry, and a newer bottling called Edwards and Chaffey Brut that has been sumptuous, but a little too variable for comfort. The Pinot Noir-Chardonnay wines are bottled under the Seaview label and can be stunning – both the NV and the vintage dated *cuvées*.

Among recent releases of the vintage-dated Seaview sparklers, which are presented in a distinctive wide-bottomed bottle (shades of Krug), the 1992 was a magnificent wine, worthy of ☆☆☆☆ – full of Champagne-like autolysis-tones and creamy, mouthfilling richness. One of the best sparkling wines yet made in Australia.

Seppelt Great Western
Great Western Victoria ☆☆☆

Like Seaview, Seppelt is owned by the Southcorp conglomerate, but the sparkling wines for which it too has long been noted are made in a slightly less classical style.

The show stopper is a burly, positively meaty sparkling wine called "Show Reserve Burgundy" in its native market. Elsewhere, the flagship export wine has been Vintage Salinger, a much leaner and more vegetal style of fizz that has won many overseas converts.

The vintage-dated Sparkling Shiraz (outstanding 1993) is made in the sweeter style, with exuberant bubbles and a nose of pure blackcurrant cordial. A cherry-fruited Great Western Brut Rosé from Pinot Noir, and honeyed all-Chardonnay Blanc de Blancs are also quietly impressive.

Taltarni Vineyards
Pyrenees Victoria ☆

A newly established sparkling wine operation on Tasmania, Clover Hill, could well expand Taltarni's portfolio in positive ways in the future, but first showings have been very sharp-textured – lean wines that seem to lack stuffing.

In Victoria, the mainstream Brut and Brut Taché (very delicately coloured *rosé*) are acceptable, if unspectacular.

Yaldara
Barossa Valley South Australia ☆

Yaldara's Reserve Brut Rosé acquires its fairly anaemic colour from a quick soak with Shiraz – simple and soundly made as is the Brut. More intriguing is the Blue Lake Ridge Sparkling Grenache, which is a hugely powerful (14.5 per cent alcohol) red sparkler, structured with considerable tannic muscle, but plenty of damson fruit to back it up and provide balance.

Yalumba
Barossa Valley South Australia ☆☆☆

One of those names that is synonymous with quality sparkling wine in Australia, Yalumba makes a versatile range of wines that offers notably good value at the lower end of the scale. The Angas Brut bottlings are its market leaders: the aromatically melony Brut; and an immensely charming strawberry scented, Shiraz-based Rosé.

Yalumba D is the premium *cuvée* – vintage-dated, full of authoritative weight and great richness of flavour (the 1994 is superb), while Cuvée One is a Pinot Noir-Chardonnay NV of biscuity sophistication and Cuvée Two is a dry but deliciously blackcurranty red fizz made from Cabernet Sauvignon.

Yellowglen Vineyards
Ballarat Victoria ☆☆☆

They are conceived as a sparkling wine specialist of Australo-Champenois parentage, Yellowglen has made tremendous advances in quality over the last decade.

Its range is a large and heterogeneous one, but pedigree is manifest throughout, this is owing in no small measure to its location in what has been considered one of Australia's most auspicious sites for sparkling wine production – the high-altitude central Victoria.

"Y" is the enigmatic name of the premium *cuvée* – a Chardonnay-Pinot Noir blend of exceptional class. The Pinot Noir-Chardonnay NV is a soft, peachy fizz; while the Vintage Brut (which is virtually three-quarters Pinot Noir) is full and weighty on the palate, and would respond well to ageing. The 1995 is particularly fine.

New Zealand

The story of New Zealand wine is one of untapped potential. Vines were first planted in the North Island in 1819 and James Busby, the first British resident, was certainly making wine by 1835. Yet it took a further 150 years for New Zealanders to appreciate that their relatively cool maritime climate offered exactly the right conditions for growing the classic vine varieties.

However, since the mid-1980s, the wine industry of New Zealand has made up for lost time – led predominently by dynamic and highly competent Australian winemakers who realised its full potential. The Marlborough district at the northern tip of the South Island, in particular, has quickly secured a reputation for excellent and highly individual still Sauvignon Blanc wine. Yet Chardonnay is much more widely planted than Sauvignon in Marlborough and throughout New Zealand. It is Chardonnay blended with fresh, long-flavoured Pinot Noir, and occasionally a little spicy, fast-maturing Pinot Meunier, which forms the classic base for New Zealand's premium, traditional-method sparkling wines. Their fine fruit-and-acid balance, enhanced by a ripe exotic character, makes them pre-eminent alternatives to Champagne.

However, these classically made-in-the-bottle products account for less than a quarter of all the sparkling wines made in New Zealand; the great majority are still made by the gas injected, tank, or transfer methods (*see* below).

New Zealand's sparkling wines are made by four different methods:-

Gas Injected/Carbonation
The cheapest base wines are gas injected with carbon dioxide. As there is no natural second fermentation in the bottle, the bubbles are not properly integrated into the wine, so the fizz rapidly evaporates in the glass.

Bulk/Charmat fermentation
A secondary fermentation of the base wine is induced in a closed tank by the catalysts of added yeasts and sugars. The bubbles are tenuously bound into the wine – the resulting *mousse* short lived.

Méthode Champenoise/Méthode Traditionelle
The classic Champagne method, where second fermentation takes place naturally and, one hopes, slowly in the bottle.

As the bubbles are created, the yeast cells in the wine are broken down by the equally natural biochemical process of autolysis. This adds a touch of complexity – often inadequately described as a biscuity taste – to the finished wine. The bubbles are persistent and last a good long time in the glass.

New Zealand's Champagne-method sparkling wines are aged in the bottle for up to three years before sale. The words "fermented in this bottle" denotes an authentic sparkling wine from New Zealand, made by the Champagne method.

Transfer method
A rapid technological gloss on the traditional method of bottle fermentation, in its final stages.

The near-finished sparkling wines are neither riddled nor disgorged; instead the wine is transferred from the bottle into hermetically sealed and pressurised tanks, where it is filtered, sugar dosed, and then rebottled. In the case of the hugely successful Lindauer (Montana) brand, it makes for a delicious and sharply priced wine.

Cellier Le Brun
Renwick ☆to☆☆

Champenois Daniel Le Brun and his New-Zealand-born wife Adèle were among Marlborough's first sparkling winemakers to plant the classic combination of the two Pinots and Chardonnay in 1980. The style of their Champagne method wines was big, broad and slightly oxidative.

The Le Bruns are no longer involved in the business. Under the new owners, the wines are more refined and elegant. The best *cuvée* is the rich and well-structured Blanc de Blancs, with its fine persistent finish.

Corbans Amadeus
Henderson ☆☆☆

This is the second largest wine company in New Zealand. Corbans make the bottle-fermented, richly flavoured, and competitively priced Amadeus Cuvée from Hawke's Bay Pinot Noir and Chardonnay grapes.

Even better value is the Verdi, Corbans' other bottled-fermented *cuvée* – remarkable finesse for little outlay.

Deutz Marlborough Cuvée
Blenheim ☆☆☆☆

A joint venture between the giant Montana group and the family owned *grande marque* Champagne Deutz, resulted in the first release of Deutz Marlborough Cuvée in 1990.

Made from a 60 per cent Chardonnay, 40 per cent Pinot Noir blend – now as then – this is an outstanding wine. It shows a racy, long, invigorating and naturally dry palate; with an end note of elegant autolytic character.

Domaine Chandon
Blenheim ☆☆☆

Recently established in 1990, this is Moët's venture in New Zealand. Masterminded by the formidable trio of Dr Tony Jordan (the MD of Domaine Chandon, Australia), Richard Geoffroy (the maker of Dom Pérignon) and Jane Hunter (qqv) who monitors the grapes.

Since the first release in 1990, the amount of Pinot Noir in the blends has steadily increased to give that supple tender character, which is a hallmark of the Moët style. The future looks very bright here.

Highfield
Blenheim ☆☆

Newly opened in 1995, this youthful Marborough winery specialises in the production of premium sparkling wines. The 1993 is a classic blend of Pinot Noir and Chardonnnay and was released in 1997. Michel Drappier, a very talented producer of Champagne in the Aube, is technical consultant.

Hunters Miru Miru
Marlborough ☆☆

The indefatigable Jane Hunter's new sparkling *cuvée*, Miru Miru, means bubbles in Maori. Aptly named, for this is a briskly sparkling wine with forward, pure and fruity flavours of Chardonnay and Pinot Noir, in a 60 to 40 per cent mix.

Lindauer-Montana
Riverlands Blenheim ☆☆☆

The Colossus of the New Zealand's wine industry, accounting for 40 per cent of production. Lindauer-Montana is run with an enlightened mix of large-scale business vision and a sleepless urge for self improvement.

Since 1989, and the association with Deutz Champagne, the quality of the best-selling Lindauer Brut has greatly improved – the proportion of Chenin Blanc in the blend has decreased in favour of more Pinot Noir and Chardonnay. Now made by the transfer method, it is an admirably clean-tasting, refreshing, and keenly priced wine.

The Lindauer Special Reserve has a delectable Pinot Noir-led flavour, from Hawke's Bay and Marlborough grapes. (*See also* Deutz Marlborough Cuvée.)

Matua Valley Wines
Waimauku ☆☆☆

An admired estate with new vineyards in the Marlborough, Gisborne and Hawke's Bay areas, which supplement the original one in Waimauku.

The Spence brothers have been making sparkling wines since 1987. They are Pinot Noir led, spending two years on the lees before *dégorgement* to reveal succulent complex flavours. Also, lovely silken-textured Sauvignon Blanc; rich, toasty Chardonnay and potentially exciting Pinot Gris.

Mills Reef Winery
Bethlehem ☆to☆☆

Paddy Preston is the patriarch of this family run winery. Based in the Bay of Plenty, but using Hawke's Bay fruit, this winery has a love affair with barrel-fermented Chardonnay, which dominates the base wine for his premium *cuvée* – the Mills Reef Traditional Method. His sharply priced Mills Reef Charisma, in contrast, is based on Pinot Noir.

These are wines with wild flavours, which you either love or hate. Character they don't lack.

Morton Estate
Katikati ☆☆☆☆

A top estate in the North Island with a wholly justified reputation for outstanding sparkling wine, and superb reds among its still wine range. Morton's greatest asset is its 70-

hectare Riverview vineyard, in a high, cool site behind Hawke's Bay. The fairly priced Sparkling Brut NV, including 20 per cent Pinot Meunier in the blend, has a delightful fresh-baked bread character, both on nose and palate.

The vintage-dated *méthode champenoise* is a brilliant Pinot Noir-led wine, with a complex style akin to Champagne, yet with a real taste of its own south Pacific home.

Nautilus Estate
Renwick ☆☆

Part of the Australian Yalumba group. A well-financed estate making promising sparkling wine from Marlborough fruit. The Pinot Noir-Chardonnay Cuvée shows attractive red-fruits flavours and fine sustaining acidity.

Parker Méthode Champenoise
Gisborne ☆☆

A boutique winery specialising in bottle-fermented sparkling wines. The top-of-the-range Classical Brut is aged for five to six years on lees before it is released. It shows a good balance of freshness and richness.

Pelorus (Cloudy Bay)
Blenheim ☆☆☆☆

The *ne plus ultra* of New Zealand's sparking wines. Pelorus is yet another resounding success from the Cloudy Bay winery whose Marlborough Sauvignon Blanc has already taken the world by storm.

The vintage 1993 Pelorus is a classic blend of Pinot Noir and Chardonnay. It is a superb and golden wine – both creamy and rich, yet impeccably balanced. The Krug of the southern hemisphere.

Selaks
Kumeu ☆☆☆

Respected white wine specialists, the Selak family make especially good Sauvignon Blanc (first-rate Founders Reserve) and traditional method sparkling wines – impressive for their elegant, fine-boned structure and reasonable price.

Both the Brut and Extra Dry are excellent.

Soljans Wines
Henderson ☆☆

Founded in 1937 and still run by the same Croatian family, this winery built a reputation for the high quality of its fortified wines (excellent well-aged "sherry").

There are two sparkling wines – the Muscat-based and sweetish Momento; plus the very respectable *méthode traditionelle* Legacy. It has fine, clean, citrussy style with excellent definition of flavour.

South Africa

The sparkling wine industry of South Africa, although in many ways still in its infancy, has made great strides over the last decade or so. As with Australia, it may have seemed something of a pipedream to attempt to produce elegant bottle-fermented fizz in a such a hot climate, and yet the efforts of the better producers have quite belied any early scepticism. The coastal Stellenbosch region has been a favoured site for sparklers because of the mitigating influence of the ocean breezes, but inland districts like Paarl, Tulbagh and even the baking Robertson Valley have improbably excelled as well.

Sparkling wines in South Africa are made using the various methods described previously – the Charmat or tank method, or even rough-and-ready carbonation, are the big sellers in the domestic market. But, where exports are concerned, these are quite rightly geared to quality products made by the traditional method, which has been given the legal title Méthode Cap Classique (MCC).

Overwhelmingly, Pinot Noir and Chardonnay are the grapes used in the production of sparkling wines, although some wineries bulk their blends with a little Chenin Blanc. The tendency has been to produce wines with relatively high *dosage* in the interests of broadening consumer appeal, but increasingly, more Champagne-like levels of Brut dryness are becoming the norm.

There is not very much *rosé* produced, but there is a surprisingly high proportion of vintage-dated wine, much of which responds exceptionally well to further ageing in bottle. Among the carbonated fizzes, a style that has become South Africa's own is cheerful, grassy sparkling Sauvignon Blanc – a highly attractive hot weather quaffer.

Frankly, arguably more than in any other non-European winemaking country, the potential for great sparkling wines in South Africa is genuinely formidable.

Graham Beck
Robertson ☆☆☆

The Robertson Valley was originally thought a more suited region to brandy production than to quality sparkling wines, but Graham Beck has lost no time in disproving that theory.

His wines are sold under his own name, and can also appear under the brand name Madeba. The basic Brut is a 50 per cent each-way blend of Pinot Noir and Chardonnay with a good autolytic toastiness; but the Blanc de Blancs, vintage-dated Chardonnay (and in particular the 1992) is in another class for its soft, creamy distinction – a quality attributed to the use of imported Champagne barrels.

Also, new is a late disgorged style called Graham Beck RD... look out, Bollinger!

Boschendal Estate
Groot Drakenstein Paarl ☆☆

Noted as one of the pioneers of MCC sparklers in the Cape, Boschendal produce a basic Brut from Pinot Noir and Chardonnay, with crisp, citric bite on the palate. Plus, an exotically fruity NV Blanc de Blancs under the label Le Grand Pavillon, where Chardonnay is supported by Sémillon.

Cabrière Estate
Franschhoek ☆☆☆

Owned by Achim von Arnim (ex-Boschendal), Cabrière's label for its sparklers is Pierre Jourdan. The star seems to be the richly yeasty Blanc de Blancs, for which a proportion of the Chardonnay is matured in Champagne oak.

The Brut impresses with good Pinot Noir depth, while the Cuvée Belle Rose (not *rosé*) is entirely from Pinot Noir. The undosed Brut Sauvage is an acid challenge to the tastebuds.

Franschhoek Vineyards
Franschhoek ☆

This is a cooperative venture whose best fizz is a carbonated, vintage Sauvignon Blanc Brut with plenty of spanking-fresh citrus flavour.

J C le Roux
Stellenbosch ☆☆

Part of the large-scale Bergkelder organisation, this estate produces ambitious MCC wines as well as more basic carbonated products.

The MCC wines take the form of a pair of vintage-dated varietal sparklers – one a vivacious Chardonnay; and the other a weighty, powerful Pinot Noir that spends four years on its lees and also ages well in the bottle.

Longridge
Stellenbosch ☆☆☆

A great leap forward in quality was made by the 1993 release of Longridge's Brut MCC sparkler, that uses equal parts Chardonnay and Pinot Noir.

It has unarguable pedigree, derived from a profound lees-influenced richness; and the 1994 is nearly as good. Fairly high *dosage* is a feature.

Nederburg
Paarl ☆

This big-volume winery makes a quietly impressive, creamy MCC Chardonnay called "Blanquette", as well as South Africa's market leading dry fizz, Première Cuvée Brut.

Made by the tank method and based on Chenin Blanc, the latter is crisp, simple and reliable.

Pongrácz
Stellenbosch ☆☆

Made, like the J C le Roux wines, by the Bergkelder group, Pongrácz was among the early pioneers of premium Cap-Classique sparkling wines.

It is a non vintage blend of two-thirds Pinot Noir, one-third Chardonnay – with good yeasty tones, and an easy-drinking, commercial fruitiness. The wine is named after the late Desiderius Pongrácz – a Hungarian-born refugee from the USSR who became one of the Bergkelder's star viticulturists.

Simonsig Estate
Stellenbosch ☆☆

The bulk-producing Simonsig can be said to have started it all by producing South Africa's first commercially marketed MCC sparkler, Kaapse Vonkel, in 1971.

Then Chenin Blanc, it is now a Pinot Noir-Chardonnay blend, with attractive hazelnut aromas and gently creamy mouthfeel. The 1992 is especially good; 1993 is not far behind.

Twee Jonge Gezellen
Tulbagh ☆☆☆☆

Winemaker Nicky Krone not only makes his own star sparkler, Krone Borealis Brut, but also is involved with the Cuvée Cap Mumm, in what is so far South Africa's only joint venture with a Champagne house.

The Krone Borealis is a vintage-dated, half and half Pinot Noir-Chardonnay blend, that achieves magisterial class despite a relatively brief ageing on lees. When given extra bottle age, it acquires the clotted-cream aroma and velvet-soft richness of good vintage Champagne. The outstanding, relatively recent vintage is the 1993.

Villiera Estate
Paarl ☆☆

Sparkling wines form the backbone of Villiera's operations, led by NV Tradition Carte Rouge, in which an idiosyncratic 15 per cent each of Pinotage and Chenin Blanc support the Pinot Noir and Chardonnay in a straightforward bone dry fizz.

The upmarket Grande Cuvée Carte d'Or is a Pinot Noir-Chardonnay blend of immense depth and complexity – acquired through long lees ageing and cellar maturation.

Vinfruco
Stellenbosch ☆☆

An export operation financed by South Africa's largest fruit dealers Unifruco, this range includes a new MCC sparkler – Oak Village Cuvée Brut. It is a lush and honeyed non vintage blend, with admirable length and complexity. If this standard is maintained, then the wine could well be worth ☆☆☆.

The rest of the world

Of the 30 or so vine growing countries in the world, there is hardly one that does not produce sparkling wine. The big players are France, Italy, Spain and Germany – accounting for 75 per cent of the total. But, California, Australia, New Zealand and South Africa increasingly challenge western Europe's dominance.

Now settle in your seats for a whirlwind tour of the globe in search of good fizz!

AUSTRIA

Austria produces over 20 million bottles of sparkling wine a year, known as sekt or *schaumweine*. Much of it is made from Welschriesling or Gruner Veltlinger grapes that are generally too low in acidity to achieve that "verve and tension" essential to a good sparkler.

However, plantings of Rhine Riesling and Pinot Blanc are increasing, and these could produce better results in the future. Presently, there is a superior type of Austrian sparkling wine called Qualitätsschaumwein, which must be made by the Charmat or Champagne method and have nine months bottle age following the *prise de mousse*.

Based in Vienna, the centre of the Austrian sparkling wine trade, two Champagne method producers stand out – Schlumberger, who age their Pinot Blanc-led Cuvée Victoria for up to 30 months before *dégorgement*. The other is the Winzerhaus Weinvertriebdges Niederösterreich, something of a mouthful to pronouce, but is a fine cooperative making the delightfully named Frizzante Furioso, which includes a good amount of Chardonnay in the blend.

BULGARIA

The wine industry in Bulgaria is no longer state controlled. Around 25-million bottles of sparkling wine (*iskra*) are made each year, the best from Riesling and Chardonnay. Labels to look for include – Magura, Balkan Cross, and Schwarze Meer.

CANADA

This is the dark horse of the wine world, currently producing some excellent still, dry and classic-method fizz.

Temperate British Columbia in the Pacific Northwest is home to Summerhill Estate and a very decent Champagne-method Riesling Brut.

Across in Ontario, there are several good traditional-fizz producers, mainly using Chardonnay.

SOUTH AMERICA

The Chileans are taking the wine shelves of supermarkets and shopping malls by storm right now, though she is a relatively small producer of sparkling wine. Now, the most important producer is Valdivieso – making a fine Grand Brut of Pinot Noir and Chardonnay, with an Australian winemaker.

On the other side of the Andes, in Mendoza, the Argentine outposts of Moët & Chandon and Piper-Heidsieck, make fine, fresh sparklers which are a cut above the average.

ENGLAND

England certainly had something to celebrate in 1997, for that summer at the International Wine and Spirit competition the gold medal for the best wine in all categories – from a field of over 30 nations – was awarded to a sparkling, traditional-method Blanc de Blancs made from pure Chardonnay grapes grown on the Kimmeridgian hills of Sussex.

The wine was a vintage 1992 from the Nyetimber vineyard in West Chiltingdon and was made by the owners, Sandy and Stuart Moss, a couple from Chicago. Their mission was to resurrect England's reputation for wine-grape growing that had stood so high in the early middle-ages – in the late 12th-century, there were 1,300 flourishing vineyards here.

The conventional wisdom that Britain is too far north to ripen grapes sufficiently to make consistently good wine, an opinion I used to share, loses much of its force when applied to sparkling wine – after all, the chalky soils of the South Downs and the long, cool growing season is similar to those of Champagne – 180-miles southeast of Calais, but still close enough to the Channel to be affected by the Gulf Stream.

Nyetimber is just one of several English vineyards making good sparkling wine, usually on chalky downland sites. Peter Hall, at Breaky Bottom just outside Lewes, is one of England's best winemakers and is developing a new sparkler from Seyval Blanc and other varieties. At Chapel Down, north of Chichester, the Epoch Brut is winning accolades. The environmentally friendly viticulture and Australian-influenced winemaking at Thames Valley Vineyard has blossomed into the first-rate Ascot Brut and Heritage.

Australians are found everywhere grapes are grown nowadays, many seeing a great future for English sparkling wines. The Aussie guru Dr Richard Smart is having a great influence on the winemaking at the excellent Three Choirs Vineyard in Gloucestershire. Denbies is the giant of English wine, with 100 hectares of chalk-hillside vineyards near Dorking. Winemaking is a bit clinical with "safe", but hardly exciting results. Denbies' range of sparkling wines, based on both German and French varieties, is certainly decent, but has quite high levels of *dosage*.

GREECE

Greece, situated between the 33rd and 41st latitudes north, has some of the hottest wine regions in the world. Yet, CAIR – the cooperative on the island of Rhodes – makes large amounts of improving sparkling wine, by the traditional method. In the village Emponas on Mount Atavisos, the Triantafyllou family has been making and trading in Rhodes wines since the mid-1960s – Emery Grand Prix Méthode Traditionelle, a five-year-old sparkler of rich-gold colour, regular bubbles and balancing acidity.

Another traditional method fizz is the elegant Villa Amalia by Tselepos in the Pelepponese.

HUNGARY

Hungary produces sparkling wine by the traditional (*pezsgo*), tank and transfer methods. Hungarians have a sweet tooth and so many of the *cuvées* are made to suit their tastes.

But, the old-established firm of Torley, near Budapest, make nearly one million bottles a year of nearly dry and respectable, traditional *pezsgo*.

INDIA

In 1982 Jean Brisbois, a Champenois oenologist from Piper-Heidsieck, began the construction of a winery at Narayangaon near Poona (financed by the Indage hotel group) to produce *methode champenoise* wines.

In 1985, the Chardonnay-led Omar Khayyam was released. It is a sparkling wine of excellent quality, with fine small bubbles and a dry, clean, delicate taste.

LUXEMBOURG

At the northernmost and coolest latitude on the European continent where vines can be grown, Luxembourg has a long history of sparkling winemaking, and its high-acid grapes have often been used by German sekt producers.

The Crémant de Luxembourg appellation was created in 1991 and is governed by the same strict rules as those for French *crémants*. The permitted grapes are Elbling, Pinot Blanc, Riesling and Pinot Noir (the latter only used for *rosé*).

The family owned firm of Bernard-Massard is the leading name in the field. Nearly 70 per cent of wine production in Luxembourg is in the hands of cooperatives. The main sales are in the Duchy itself and bordering Benelux countries.

PORTUGAL

Bordering the Atlantic, Portugal has a more propitious climate for sparkling wine production than Spain, but has been much less successful than her richer neighbour – due to a lack of modern technology.

However, since Portugal's entry to the European Union and development grants from Brussels, recent plantings of Chardonnay and a little Pinot Noir in the main production regions of Bairrada (between Oporto and Lisbon) and Lamengo (at the mouth of the Douro River), all bode well for the future. The best of Portugal's Champagne method wines are made by wealthy companies with the right sparkling wine technology already in place. For example, the Pinot Noir- and Chardonnay-based Velha Reserva Raposeira Brut, a brand owned by Seagrams, is well up to the standard of the better cavas of Spain.

Sogrape, the makers of Mateus Rosé, has intelligently diversified its wine interests and now produces some very respectable bottle-fermented bubbly in Bairrada, mainly from indigenous Portuguese grapes like Maria Gomez. Luis Pato also makes a wide range of very good sparkling wines in this region, from the Baga grape.

THE RUSSIAS (FORMER USSR)

The Russians drink prodigious quantities of sparkling wine (*shampanskoye*), much of it very sweet.

Before the Bolshevik revolution of 1917, the imperial court at St Petersburg was the main customer of such great Champagne houses as Veuve Clicquot and Louis Roederer. And post 1989, Russia is a promising new market once again – assuming the bills will be paid.

The Russias are important producers of fizz in their own right, producing 250 million bottles a year by the tank and continuous flow methods. It is hard to talk about quality, as the wines are nearly all drunk at home.

SWITZERLAND

Switzerland makes some very good still white and red wines from indigenous grapes, but the sparklers are made from a hotchpotch of local and imported grapes.

Far and away the best Swiss producer is Mauler & Cie at Motiers, close to the border with France. A blending of Pinot Noir and Chardonnay; hand riddling and long ageing make this an excellent source of traditional method wines to rival the best Crémant de Jura – produced nearby.

Glossary

Appellation d'Origine Contrôlée (AOC) the certificate of authenticity for French wine of a higher quality; to gain this status the wine must conform to rules regarding its exact provenance and methods of production (*see also* DO, Spain; DOC and DOCG, Italy; QbA, Germany).

Aroma strictly speaking, this tasting term applies to the fruity scent of young wine, rather than the more mature smell or "bouquet" of older wine. In practice, the two terms are interchangeable.

Assemblage the blending of wines. In Champagne it may also refer to the ratio of grapes (eg 60 per cent Chardonnay, 40 per cent Pinot Noir) that make up the final blend or *cuvée*.

Atmospheres the measurement of atmospheric pressure – one atmosphere = 15 pounds per square inch.

Autolysis the biochemical process in which the yeast cells are broken down. In Champagne production it begins during the *prise de mousse* (qv), slowly adding a vital complexity to the finished taste over the course of the wine's ageing period in bottle.

Autolytic a technical tasting term applied to a Champagne which shows a yeasty or biscuit-like secondary flavour, usually the result of extended ageing in bottle.

Balance an important and very useful tasting term to describe a wine, usually of high quality, in which the natural elements of acids, alcohol, fruit and tannins meld harmoniously.

Barrique a small oak barrel of 225 litres (approximately 50 gallons) capacity.

Blanc de Blancs a sparkling wine made entirely from white grapes. A pure Chardonnay Champagne.

Blanc de Noirs a sparkling wine made entirely from black grapes, usually Pinot Noir.

Bulk (Charmat or Cuve Close) method an efficient way of making sparkling wine, suitable for high volume production. A second fermentation is induced in a tank by adding the catalyst of yeasts and sugar. The resulting bubbles are tenuously bound into the wine and are relatively short lived.

Buyer's Own Brand (BOB) used especially by British wine merchants, retail chains and supermarkets requiring their own label rather than that of the producer who makes the Champagne for them. A BOB can be recognised by the initials MA (*marque d'acheteur*) found at the bottom right-hand corner of the label.

Cantina the Italian word for cellar or winery.

Cantina Sociale an Italian wine cooperative.

Carbonated or gas-injection method the most basic and least satisfactory way of making sparkling wine. Carbonic gas (carbon dioxide) is injected into the wine; with no natural fermentation in bottle or tank, the bubbles are not properly integrated into the wine and vanish rapidly in an open bottle.

Champagne or traditional method the classic way of making sparkling wine, in which a natural fermentation takes place in the bottle resulting in well integrated bubbles in the wine (*prise de mousse*). When this is conducted slowly, and following an extended ageing period in bottle, the bubbles should be small, lasting a very long time in the glass.

Cava a DO Spanish sparkling wine made by the traditional method; over 95 per cent is produced in the Penedès district of Barcelona Province (Catalonia).

Cave a cellar, usually underground in Champagne.

Chef de caves a cellar master, or technical director, in charge of Champagne production; usually a highly qualified *oenologist* (wine scientist) responsible for blending.

Cold settling a technically advanced technique of *débourbage* (qv) in which unfermented grape juice ("must") is completely cleared of any solid matter and colouring elements by refrigeration. A great boon for Champagne makers wanting the purest possible flavours in their finished wines. James Coffinet, the *chef de caves* at Pol Roger, was the pioneer of cold settling in his previous post at Billecart-Salmon.

Coopérative-Manipulante (CM) a cooperative making and selling Champagne.

Coteaux Champenois an AOC for still white, *rosé* and red wine produced in the Champagne winefield. Known as Vin Nature de Champagne before 1973.

Crayères the Gallo-Roman chalk pits found in Reims, used as Champagne cellars.

Crémant in Champagne, traditionally a gently sparkling wine with about 3.5 atmospheres. Since August 1994, the word may not appear on the main label of a Champagne bottle. The official use of the term *crémant* is reserved for AOC sparkling wines made by the traditional method in Alsace, the Loire, Burgundy, the Rhône (Die), Limoux, Bordeaux and the Jura.

Cuvée 1.the final Champagne blend. 2.the first pressings (the best part) of the grapes in Champagne producing 2,050 litres of juice.

Débourbage a decantation or separation of pressed grape juice from solid matter prior to fermentation.

Dégorgement the removal of the deposit or lees from a bottle of Champagne caused by the second fermentation.

Dégorgement à la glace the most common method of disgorging in which the bottle passes neck down through a bath of freezing brine and the deposit, imprisoned in a "sorbet" of near-frozen ice, is expelled on removal of the cork or crown cap.

Dégorgement à la volée the classic method of disgorging by hand without freezing; rarely used nowadays, although in the case of old Champagnes it is the best way as it does not impair the bouquet of the wines.

Demi-muid an old oak cask of 600 litres (132 gallons).

DO the Spanish equivalent of French AOC (*see* AOC).

DOC or DOCG the Italian equivalent of French AOC (*see* AOC), the rules of DOCG being more demanding.

Dosage a dose of sugar and wine added to Champagne or sparkling wine to soften the impact of the wine's acidity prior to release. It is expressed in percentages or grammes of sugar per litre of wine.

Echelle des Crus the classification of the Champagne *crus* or "ladder of growths" formulated after the First World War and expressed on a percentage scale. It is geographically based, but is essentially an index of price, based on the reputed quality of grapes from specific vineyards and hillsides. Deuxièmes Crus rate 80-89 per cent; Premiers Crus 90-99 per cent; Grands Crus 100 per cent.

Foudre a large wooden cask of no fixed size. Used to store reserve wines by traditionalist Champagne makers.

Frizzante an Italian word used to describe slightly sparkling wines such as Moscato d'Asti or Freisa (*see also* Pétillant).

Grand Cru one of 17 Champagne villages rated at 100 per cent on the *échelle des crus*.

Girasol or gyropalette an automatic, computer-controlled riddling machine whose *palette* (or metal cage) holds up to 500 bottles.

Grande Marque until 1997, this was a leading Champagne house that belonged to an association of 23 member firms; now officially defunct, though the term is likely to be used for some years yet.

Hybrids mongrel grapes that are usually a cross between classic *vinifera* and tougher *labrusca* types. The best one is Seyval Blanc, a French hybrid.

Lees the sediment or deposit that accumulates in the bottom of a tank or (in the case of Champagne) on the inner sides of a bottle as the by-product of fermentation; largely composed of dead yeasts which add complexity to a Champagne's flavour (*see* Autolysis).

Malolactic fermentation the conversion of tart malic acid into milder lactic acid to make wines softer but also more complex in style.

Méthode champenoise the "Champagne method", or the traditional way of making Champagne and other quality sparkling wines by a second fermentation. Under EU rules, the term is being progressively outlawed, and replaced by terms like *méthode traditionelle*.

Metodo classico the Italian term for traditionally bottle-fermented sparkling wine.

Méthode dioise an adaptation of the *méthode rurale*. Employed exclusively in the making of Clairette de Die, involving several months of long, cold fermentations before the wines are bottled.

Millésime the French word for a (released) vintage of Champagne.

Millésimé the French word meaning vintage-dated.

Monocru a Champagne which is produced from a single *cru* (commune or village).

Mousse bubbles!

Mousseux a fully sparkling wine of five to six atmospheres.

Negociant-Manipulant (NM) a merchant who is permitted to buy his grapes or wines for his *cuvées* from other sources. Some or all of the wines in a blend may come from the NM's own vineyards. All the *grandes marques* are NMs.

NV an abbreviation for non vintage.

Pétillant slightly sparkling wines eg Vouvray Pétillant.

Premier Cru in Champagne a winegrowing commune rated between 90 and 99 per cent on the *échelle des crus*.

Prise de Mousse the second fermentation in bottle, causing the wine to sparkle.

Pupitres inverted wooden racks with holes in them, thus designed for the process of *remuage* (riddling).

Quälitswein bestimmter Anbaugebiete (QbA) German quality wine of authenticated provenance.

Récoltant-Coopérateur (RC) a small grower without the means to vinify Champagne, who has it made from his own grapes by one or more cooperatives and sells the finished Champagne under his own label. Champagne labelled RC is not truly a grower's wine as grapes from the *récoltant-coopérateur* may be blended with others.

Récemment Dégorgé (RD) "recently disgorged", this term usually applies to a very high quality, long aged vintage Champagne that has been disgorged no more than two or three months before release. The term RD has been patented by Bollinger, who is recognised as the leading producer of late released Champagne.

Récoltant-Manipulant (RM) a grower making Champagne from his own grapes.

Remuage "riddling", the inverted bottles of sparkling wine are turned every day so that the deposit may slide down and settle on the cork or temporary closure.

Reserve wines older wines than those from the current vintage kept "in reserve" to bring balance and maturity to a Champagne blend.

Schaumwein the most basic type of German or Austrian sparkling wine.

Sekt a superior type of German sparkling wine.

Spumante an Italian sparkling wine of five atmospheres.

Sur Lattes 1.Champagnes stored (binned) on their sides. 2.Near-finished Champagnes which are sold on by the producer and labelled as the buyer's own product.

Taille the second pressings of Champagne grapes, generally giving wines of lesser quality. However, the better part of the Chardonnay *taille* can give a blend some early fruitiness.

Toques et Clochers the Limoux equivalent of the Hospices de Beaune, awarding labels to especially good Chardonnays.

Transfer method involves secondary fermentation in bottle, after which the resulting wine is cleaned up in tank, obviating the need for *dégorgement*.

Tête de Cuvée, Coeur de Cuvée the finest juice from the first pressings of the *cuvée*. Some grower-Champagne makers claim that the best juice is the middle part of the *cuvée* "the heart" at the point where 1,600–1,800 litres (out of a total of 2,050 litres) has been drawn off.

Vendange vintage.

Vignaoili a wine grower (Italy).

Vigneron a wine grower (France).

Vitis labrusca a non-classic, hardy, weather-resistant family of vines with an often sickly, foxy smell (eg the Concord grape). Still grown in the USA, and used in sparkling wine blends outside California and Oregon.

Vitis vinifera the classic winemaker's vine, reputedly first found in the Trancauscasian region of what is modern Armenia c 7,000 BC. Great sparkling wine grapes like Pinot Noir and Chardonnay, as well as Riesling and Chenin Blanc, belong to this family.

Champagne vintage guide

In 1879, the journalist Henry Vizetelly wrote that a truly great Champagne vintage never occurs more than twice in a decade, and that over the same period there are usually two quite good ones. More than a century on, Vizetelly's axiom is still broadly true. However, the Champagne houses and particularly growers tend to release a vintage too often and in unsuitable years.

This guide points you to the true vintages back to 1964, the oldest year occasionally available at auction and still drinking well, if carefully stored. Genuine vintage years are described and rated on a star-rating system, as explained below. Intervening years are also described but not rated (ie do not have any stars).

For the collector interested in really old Champagne, there are brief notes made about important vintages pre-1964 back to 1900. No attempt is made to star rate these golden oldies, if necessary just question any specialist wine merchant or stockholder closely about where the venerable bottle comes from and how it has been stored.

The star-rating system used here is as follows:

☆☆☆☆ outstanding; truly great

☆☆☆ excellent; a classic; much admired

☆☆ good, well-balanced year

☆ decent year needing careful selection; ask an expert for advice if in doubt

rating in brackets eg (☆☆) drink up, possibly over the hill

1997 Following a dreadful summer with every conceivable problem in the vineyard, the vintage was saved by brilliant September weather. Results were ripe but low-acid wines, and good for blending with the formidably structured 1996s.

1996 ☆☆☆☆ Champagnes of monumental structure, high in alcohol and acidity, needing many years to reach maturity. Old growers compare this to 1928. A great vintage for the patient.

1995 ☆☆☆ Classic, finely balanced wines; a Chardonnay year *par excellence.*

1994 A large crop spoilt by heavy rain at vintage time. Strictly for the blending vats.

1993 ☆☆ The best vintage in the lean period of 1991–5; aromatic, delicate, clean flavours. Very good Jacquesson Blanc de Blancs and excellent Dom Pérignon.

1992 Released by several houses, and quite a number of cooperatives and growers. Why? The wines lack body, vigour, length of flavour, and may fade quickly. Avoid.

1991 ☆ Eclipsed by the dramatic 1990, this is actually not a bad vintage, quite well balanced with good acidity. The Pommery 1991 is recommended.

1990 ☆☆to☆☆☆☆ Quite a teaser. The big houses trumpet this vintage as one of the greatest of recent decades, no doubt with millennium sales in mind. Keep a cool head. This was one of the hottest and largest vintages on record, and quality is more variable than received wisdom will admit. Producers who did not keep the acidity levels in their wines at a safely high level (ie by avoiding malolactic fermentation) have seen their Champagnes mature too rapidly, they may be over the hill by late 1999. However, the best 1990s – Billecart-Salmon, Pol Roger, Bollinger, Charles Heidsieck, Roederer Cristal – are great rich wines with years of life ahead of them.

1989 ☆☆☆ A lovely rich vintage of ripe expressive flavours that matured early; yet the best wines will mature well and be at their peak for the millennium. Bollinger Grande Année is Champagne of the vintage; Roederer Cristal, Veuve Clicquot (straight vintage) Deutz Blanc de Blancs, and Tarlant Cuvée Louis are all splendid.

1988 ☆☆☆ A classic vintage, initially dry and anything but showy. The best get better and better; their fine acidity is likely to ensure a long distinguished life. Pol Roger Cuvée Spéciale PR and Jacquesson Signature are exceptional.

1987 Not a true vintage year, though both Pommery and Jacques Selosse Cuvée d'Origine are fine Champagnes.

(1986) ☆ Released by several houses; a fast-maturing vintage that gave pleasure in its prime, but most wines are past their best. One still alive and kicking is Duval-Leroy's Cuvée des Roys.

1985 ☆☆☆☆ Small is beautiful. A tiny crop due to spring frosts produced wonderfully concentrated Champagnes, particularly those with a high Pinot Noir content. Pol Roger Cuvée Sir Winston Churchill, Laurent-Perrier Grand Siècle *exceptionellement millésime* and Bollinger RD are magnificent.

1984 Dry, lean wines; generally to be avoided, though de Castellane Commodore Rosé was good.

1983 ☆☆☆ A classic year of ripeness and good acidity, generally underrated. The best wines, especially the pure Chardonnays like Charles Heidsieck Cuvée des Millénaires are still very good.

1982 ☆☆☆☆ One of the two greatest vintages of the 1980s, wines of breathtaking beauty and class shaped by perfectly ripe Chardonnay. Krug, Dom Pérignon (both Brut and Rosé), and Pol Roger are in their prime, though the lesser wines lack acidity and are past their best.

1981 ☆☆to☆☆☆ A small crop; but fine, concentrated flavours among top wines like Krug, Bollinger, and Roederer, which still show plenty of life.

1980 ☆ Mixed-quality, high-acid wines, but those that were carefully vinified are very respectable. Fine Dom Pérignon.

1979 ☆☆☆ A vintage of great breed and lingering flavours; the initial fierce acidity has allowed the wines to mature slowly over 20 years; and the finest, such as Salon, are now at their apogee.

1978 Diffuse, clumsy wines that have not improved with age.

1977 Generally poor and thin. Roederer Cristal was the exception.

1976 ☆☆☆ The wines of this hot and bountiful year were at first criticised for their low acid levels. Yet, the best – rich in alcohol and extract – have turned out to be very long-lived Champagnes. Krug and Heidsieck Monopole Diamant Bleu are still sensational, if you can find them.

1975 ☆☆☆☆ An absolute classic year of superb balance and breed. Although less weighty and powerful than 1976, the vintage has a finer structure and the top wines show extraordinary finesse and freshness after more than 20 years ageing. Both Bollinger RD and Dom Pérignon are very good.

1974 A large crop of average quality, useful for blending. Some good *rosés* were produced.

1973 ☆☆☆ Stylish, aromatic wines with a good fruit and acid balance. Much longer lived than first expected. Krug is still excellent.

1972 A huge crop of sharp, thin wines. Awful!

1971 ☆☆☆ A small crop of classic harmonious wines that matured slowly and gracefully. Very hard to find now.

1970 (☆☆☆) For many years these were rich stylish wines, though any that are left should be consumed quickly.

1969 ☆☆to☆☆☆ High acidity in these wines gave them a very long life. Salon, the great Blanc de Blanc from Le Mesnil, is still finely austere and a great wine to match sea trout.

1968 Sour, unripe grapes made very acid wines. Generally unattractive; although some growers made some decent, pure Chardonnay Champagnes.

1967 Released as a vintage by a few houses. Nothing special and now over the hill.

1966 ☆☆☆ A small harvest of concentrated, firm, and durably structured wines that still provide great pleasure, especially the straight vintage bottlings of Bollinger and Louis Roederer. Salon is an extraordinarily rich wine with a whiff, would you believe, of *foie gras*.

1964 ☆☆☆☆ One of the greatest vintages of the second half of the century. Krug and Salon (the best) are still full of life, vigour, and endless complexities. The last year that Dom Pérignon (also wonderful) was fermented in wood.

GOOD OLDER VINTAGES:

1962 Supple, subtle and distinguished.

1959 Powerful, rich and long lived; akin to 1976.

1955 Elegant, fine and balanced.

1953 Full bodied; rich in alcohol; pure flavoured.

1952 Class in a glass; exquisite, especially Pol Roger.

1949 Classic, poised, with fine sustaining acidity.

1947 Blockbuster-style; astonishingly rich.

1945 Monumental and exceptionally long lived.

1943 Classic; refined; harmonious.

1942 Good sound vintage, after long lean run.

1934 Finesse and balance. A true vintage year.

1929 Opulent; very fine; universally released.

1928 Very great; long lived; legendary.

1925 Small crop, high quality.

1923 Small harvest, classic year.

1921 Great vintage, opulent yet balanced.

1920 Below average yields, but good quality.

1919 Normal-sized harvest; classic, well balanced, long lived.

1915 Big harvest, excellent vintage quality.

1914 Poignant vintage, paid for with the lives of women and children who picked the grapes; fine elegant wines.

1911 Great, long lived, outstanding; small harvest.

1906 Average-sized harvest, good vintage quality.

1904 Great wines of exemplary breed; bumper harvest.

1900 Bountiful year of first-class, strongly constituted wines of great quality.

Champagne gastronomique

Not so long ago the Champagne district appeared to be a gastronomic desert. In 1968, when I first worked in Epernay, there was one decent place to eat regularly – the Restaurant de la Gare – and for special occasions, the Royal Champagne at Champillon, then the only Michelin-starred restaurant for miles around. In terms of natural produce, Champagne has never been a land of plenty. Apart from good trout fished from the Marne's tributaries, the pig and the sheep were for many years the main traditional staples of the table and the base for the region's three best-known dishes: *pieds de cochons à la Ste-Ménehould* (pig's trotters grilled in breadcrumbs and *beurre fondant*); *potée champenoise* (slow-simmered casserole of salted ham, pork, mutton, and vegetables) and *andouilettes de Troyes* (chitterling sausages made from mutton).

Such rustic food has led cookery writers to claim that Champagne lacks a recognisable *cuisine* of its own and that the *répertoire* is rather limited. This is only really true in the academic sense of a strictly local culinary tradition.

Champagne does of course have a *cuisine*, drawing on the superb meat and fish from the Paris markets, on excellent fruit and vegetables from the Ile de France, and on splendid characterful cheeses such as Maroilles, Brie, Explorateur and Chaource made at the outer limits of the province. Moreover, since the 1970s talented and open-minded chefs have come to work in Reims and its surrounding area, attracted by the challenge of creating refined dishes to match the supreme subtlety of the wine for a very sophisticated clientele – the expensively suited men and women whose job is to sell Champagne around the world.

Here I give a personal selection of a dozen favourite restaurants in the Marne, the Aisne and the Aube districts; which aims to show the range, vitality and inventiveness of the *cuisine* of Champagne in the late 1990s.

The star-rating system is used similarly as before:
☆☆☆☆ outstanding cooking, worth a long journey
☆☆☆ excellent, often exceptional cooking
☆☆ good, above average cooking
☆ decent basic cooking

☆☆☆ **Auberge de Ste-Maure**
D78 10150 Ste-Maure
Tel (0)3 25 76 90 41
Seven kilometres north of Troyes by the D78 brings you to this delightful riverside restaurant which sports the rosette-winning cooking of Thierry Grandeclaude.

His talent is to put a personal touch on old favourites such as *andouilettes de Troyes* served with Chaource butter; roast turbot with a *jus* of ginger and basil; and the sonorously named *pain perdu d'epices aux poires*, a French version of bread-and-butter pudding. Excellent value, especially the *prix fixe* menus.

☆☆ Au Petit Comptoir

17 rue du Mars 51100 Reims
tel (0)3 26 40 58 58
This is a fashionable meeting place, a stylish *fin-du-siècle* bistro offers "French grandmother's cooking", but adapted to modern tastes. The *bouillabaisse* of Rascasse and the *navarin* of lamb (served May to June) are excellent. Plus, good wines at realistic prices. Book ahead.

☆☆☆to☆☆☆☆ Les Berceaux

13 rue des Berceaux 51200 Epernay
Tel (0)3 26 55 28 84
The venerable Les Berceaux hotel, all '50s flock wallpaper and creaking plumbing, was bought in 1997 by the very talented chef Patrick Michelon and his wife, Lydie. After various stages in the greatest kitchens of France, Patrick – an Alsatian – became head chef of Aux Armes de Champagne at L'Epine, and gained a Michelin star for his cooking during a ten year stint. Since becoming his own boss in Epernay, he has shown exceptional culinary imagination and range.

His *carte*, which changes three or four times a year, takes advantage of the best seasonal produce – milk-fed-Pyrenean baby lamb with the first new potatoes at Easter; *tartare* of red tuna on a *carpaccio* of monkfish for the hot days of summer; black truffles braised in white Coteaux Champenois de Chouilly in late October; veal's kidneys with a potato galette and Pinot Noir sauce all year.

There is also a wine-bar bistro offering delicious food (try the *carbonnade* of milk-fed piglet) from the same great kitchen at reasonable prices. The staff are young, enthusiastic and very professional. If you only have time for one meal in Champagne – eat here. Superb.

☆☆ Bistro du Pont

5 place General de Gaulle 10150 Pont-Ste-Marie
Tel (0)3 25 80 90 99
A warm welcome and broad smiles greet you at this bright and spotlessly clean little bistro three kilometres east of Troyes by the N77.

Their specialities include fresh salads, good steaks, great *frites*, well-kept cheeses; and good, young wines *en pichet* are also what to expect. Then, with your coffee, why not indulge in a glass of Prunelle de Troyes – a delicious plum brandy, which is made by an old distiller in the shadow of the Troyes Cathedral.

☆☆ **Château de Fère**
02130 Fère-en-Tardenois
Tel (0)3 23 82 21 13
This is definitely an impressive *château* with lovely grounds.
Unfortunately the *cuisine*, after a change of chef, was more
noticeable for its fine presentation than for memorable
flavours, on the one occasion I ate here in spring 1997. The
service is a bit stiff and formal.

☆☆ **Chez Pierrot**
16 rue de la Fauville 51100 Epernay
tel (0)3 26 55 16 93
A miniscule, picture-filled restaurant in a quiet street where
Pierre Trouillard's *bourgeois* cooking wins high marks for true
flavours at low prices.

☆☆☆ **Hotel de l'Angleterre**
19 place Mgr Tissier 51000 Châlons-en-Champagne
Tel (0)3 28 68 21 51
A solid, comfortable hotel with Michelin-starred restaurant
that every good-sized French provincial town should have.
Jacky Michel's cooking is a delight – an excellent rack of lamb
with a rosemary-infused sauce; and an especially refreshing
plate of apple desserts in various guises.

Lovely *croissants* for breakfast. Very reasonable prices for
this level of quality.

☆☆☆ **La Cote 108**
N44 02190 Berry-au-Bac
Tel (0)3 23 79 95 04
Situated 20 kilometres north of Reims by the N44, this is
where the Remois go when they want to eat really well.

Serge Courville uses the finest ingredients to create an
exceptional harmony of flavours in such offerings as warm
foie gras in a salt crust, scallops with white-port vinegar, or
crepinette of pigs trotters and lentils. There is also a range of
great wines at fair prices.

☆☆☆☆ **Les Crayères**
64 boulvard Henri-Vasnier 51100 Reims
Tel (0)3 26 82 80 80
A jewel of the Relais et Châteaux association, this 1900 town
house with its splendid park is an apt setting for the world-
class cooking of Gerard Boyer.

Based around fish dishes with inventive combinations
that excel – *ravioli* of lobster with sweetbreads; grilled sea
bass with steamed vegetables and coriander; fillet of roasted
turbot with celery and peppers braised in chicken stock – all
merit a long journey to experience. Sumptuous bedrooms.
Very high prices.

☆☆☆ Le Foch
37 boulevard Foch 51100 Reims
Tel (0)3 26 47 48 22

In the city centre close to the Place d'Erlon, Le Foch is the best place in Reims to try subtle and refined treatments of the freshest fish – fortunately, without needing a mortgage to pay the bill.

Particularly good are the *grand pot-au-feu de la mer*, the perfectly executed little escalopes of monkfish, or fillet of turbot with oysters – and to finish a *sablé* of red fruits with a lemon flavoured cream. Service can be a little artless.

☆☆☆ La Garenne
N31 51370 Champigny-sur-Vesle
Tel (0)3 26 08 26 62

It is a mystery why this excellent restaurant, close to Reims Golf Club, should have lost a star in the 1997 Michelin guide.

Chef Laurent Laplaige offers lunches that are great value for money and dinners of distinction. Fine dishes include a "marmite" of turbot, langoustines and lobster, and filet of beef with a bone-marrow and red Cumières-wine sauce. Leave room for the *tout chocolat* dessert!

☆☆☆ Le Grand Cerf
N51 51500 Rilly-la-Montagne
Tel (0)3 26 08 26 62

A handsome inn with an attractive terrace and garden, on the main N51 Reims to Epernay road.

They offer rich classical *cuisine*, tempered with a light touch. Particularly recommended are *tourte* of scallops with green asparagus and pig's trotter stuffed with sweetbreads. Outstanding wine list explained by a first class *sommelier*.

☆☆ Le Mesnil
2 rue Pasteur 51190 Le Mesnil-sur-Oger
tel (0)3 26 57 95 51

Traditional French *cuisine* – mostly fish and game – and an impressive list of Chardonnay Champagnes as you would expect in the heart of the Côte des Blancs.

☆☆☆ Le Parc de Villeneuve
N71 10110 Bar-sur-Seine
Tel (0)3 25 29 16 80

The brothers Bruno and Christophe Caironi opened this handsome restaurant, set in its own leafy park, in 1994. It has been a godsend in the gastronomic desert of the southern Aube.

Chef Bruno trained with the great Alain Ducasse in Monaco, and his cooking (awarded a Michelin star in 1997) shows fondness of Mediterranean flavours, always tempered by a sense of classical balance. The Charteuse of langoustines is a winner, as are the milk-fed veal's sweetbreads and the *soufflés*. Also, this is a good place to try the best growers' Champagnes of the Aube.

☆☆☆ **Royal Champagne**
N2051 51160 Champillon
Tel (0)3 26 52 87 11

This Relais et Châteaux hotel restaurant has magnificent views over the Marne Valley. The kitchen has maintained very high standards for 30 years, which is a rarity in the restaurant business.

Here you can be sure of a warm welcome and precisely timed, imaginative, consistent cooking. Don't miss the Bresse chicken *en croute de fleur de sel*, or the medaillons of rabbit *à la royale*. A superb wine list. And also, 27 luxury bedrooms – most with that spectacular view.

☆☆ **Table Kobus**
3 rue Dr Rousseau 51150 Epernay
tel (0)3 26 51 53 53

This was formerly the "Au Petit Comptoir" restaurant in Epernay, bought out by the head waiter and partners.

A stylish bistro, that serves above-average food, very attractively. Friendly service.